A SOCIAL HISTORY
OF MUSEUMS

A SOCIAL HISTORY
OF MUSEUMS

What the Visitors Thought

KENNETH HUDSON

First published 1975 by
THE MACMILLAN PRESS LTD
London and Basingstoke
Associated companies in New York
Dublin Melbourne Johannesburg and Madras

SBN 333 14441 4

Photoset, printed and bound
in Great Britain by
REDWOOD BURN LIMITED
Trowbridge & Esher

CONTENTS

ACKNOWLEDGEMENTS

This book owes its existence and its philosophy to the discussions, and sometimes arguments, I have had over many years with my friends who are actively engaged in running museums and in making them more useful and interesting to the public. It is a pleasure to express my particular gratitude to Robert Vogel and Eugene Ostroff, of the Smithsonian Institution, Washington; Frank Atkinson, of Beamish, the Open-Air Museum for the North East; Neil Cossons, of the Ironbridge Gorge Museum Trust; Walter Muir Whitehill, formerly of the Boston Atheneum; Sigvard Strandh, of the Technical Museum, Stockholm; Thomas Leavitt, of the Merrimack Valley Textile Museum, North Andover, Massachusetts; Jerzy Jasiuk, of the National Technical Museum, Warsaw; Anders Jespersen, of the National Museum, Copenhagen; and Wilfred Seaby, formerly of the Ulster Museum, Belfast. Their advice, their humanity and their historical perspective have been invaluable to me.

I am grateful to the various museum authorities and others who have allowed me to reproduce the photographs they supplied.

I should also like to acknowledge my indebtedness to Ann Nicholls, my collaborator on *The Directory of Museums*, who has helped me throughout in the discovery and selection of material for the present book, and in the preparation of the typescript.

August 1974   K.H.

INTRODUCTION

THE CHANGING IDEA OF
A MUSEUM

'A museum', says the International Council of Museums, 'is a permanent establishment administered in the public interest, with a view to conserve, study, exploit by various means and, basically, to exhibit, for the pleasure and education of the public, objects of cultural value.'

This definition has taken a long time to grow and even today there is considerable disagreement as to the relative importance of its various elements. It raises almost as many problems as it solves and it can mean very different things to different people. What, for example, is a 'permanent' establishment (or collection)? Is the museum of the Research Institute of Industrial Safety in Tokyo, for instance, to be considered a true museum? It undoubtedly has an educational purpose, it employs professional staff and it devotes great efforts to making its exhibits intelligible to the public. But its collections are not permanent in the sense that those of the Science Museum in London are. The exhibits are not fixed for several years at a time but are continuously being brought up to date. New devices, new ideas, new recommendations are always filtering in, exactly as they are at the Museum of Science and Industry in Chicago, where nothing is regarded as permanent either. Museums of this type seem to call for a new name, to safeguard their integrity and their right to an honest life. The new term 'expo-museums' suits them very well.

What, again, is 'the public interest'? Who decides what, at any given moment, the public interest may be? By what yardstick is the cultural value of an object measured? What proportion of the museum's funds, energy and space is to be given

I

to each of its aims? Is it a place primarily for scholars or primarily for the general public? Does the staff see it as a kind of university-annexe or as a high-grade exhibition or pleasure-drome?

A year or two before he retired, the very experienced Public Relations Officer at the Victoria and Albert Museum in London, Charles Gibbs-Smith, hit out in public against the professional museum world. Many museum curators, he wrote, 'either patronise, resent, despise, dislike or even hate the public.'[1] New entrants to the profession, he said, picked up this attitude very early in their career.

> The general attitude now apparently encouraged in the rising generation of museum staffs tends to take them even further away from the desire to feel and communicate enthusiasm for the objects in their charge, and also further away from any obligation to share their knowledge with the public. They want to feel that they are among the élite of museum mortals, perpetually engaged in the more rarified regions of research. It is such a pity that first their teachers and then their Directors fail to tell them that their research is often little short of phoney; or, at best, that it should take a decidedly second place in their Museum work.[2]

Museum staffs, he believed, had been caught up in the academic rat-race. Listening to his art-history-trained colleagues, he found it 'hard to believe that they are talking about works of art at all. They seem terrified of talking with affection or enthusiasm about a painting, or sculpture, or piece of magnificent furniture.'[3] Was this 'for fear of appearing vulgar or common', or 'of losing their status as serious scholars'?

It is not easy to say how widespread this situation is, although anyone who spends much time talking to people in the museum field, or who attends museum conferences, is well aware that it is certainly to be found to some extent at all the large museums. The present writer recalls an occasion in 1972 when he was told by the Director of one of the most famous art museums in Vienna that it would be no bad thing if the doors of the museum were kept permanently closed, so that prospective visitors would have to produce satisfactory evidence of their fitness to be admitted. Government policy unfortunately forbade this, and the public was allowed entry unscreened. The Director himself, a noted scholar, gave gallery-lectures from time to time. They made no concessions to the lay mind, but it is impossible to say whether they were appreciated or understood, because no attempt was made to find out. Asked about this, the Director said he thought it was very likely that he was casting pearls before swine, but it was a situation he accepted. He certainly had no intention of wasting museum funds on such frivolous activities as surveys aimed at discovering the reactions of the visitors to his museum, or of the audiences at his lectures. The public should consider itself fortunate to have the opportunity to see the masterpieces the building contained.

No doubt some of the visitors took the same view; but, in the absence of any properly conducted research one can only rely on impressions and overheard comments. During the summer months, coachloads of Russian tourists arrive daily at the Zwinger in Dresden. Most of them are very ordinary working-class men and women, but they are taken round the picture collections as if they were all art historians, with a substantial mini-lecture in front of the major paintings. The expression on their faces rarely changes as the guide moves relentlessly from detail to detail, they never ask questions and they take no notes. What, in fact, are they getting out of the whole business? Is it necessary that they should understand what they are being given? Is it, perhaps, sufficient that they shall realise that they are in the presence of what are officially recognised as great works of art? Does their respectful, if uncomprehending, attendance make it easier for the art historians to hold down their jobs and draw on public funds for its purpose? Is it all, as Mr Gibbs-Smith suggests, a professional conspiracy, very much against the public interest?

The argument has been going on for a long time. It is rooted in an old-established belief, the product of an aristocratic and hierarchical society – that art and scholarship are for a closed circle. The public may admire in a general way, but it should realise its permanent and unchangeable inferiority and keep its distance. In Europe, museums and art galleries began at a time when the people who owned and ran them had a contempt for the masses. Collections were formed by men who wished to display them to others with the same tastes and level of knowledge as themselves, for connoisseurs and scholars. Any idea that there might be a duty to make this material attractive or intelligible to a broader range of people would have seemed ludicrous.

In the seventeenth century only distinguished travellers and foreign scholars were, as a rule, allowed to see the collections belonging to the European princes, which were often housed in the palace itself. After 1700, groups of visitors were guided round the Imperial Gallery in Vienna, but were required to pay 12 guilders a group – a huge sum for the time – to the curator, who needed the money in order to supplement his very poor salary. In Vienna, as elsewhere, when a wider range of people began to claim the right to visit these great collections, and to do so without paying a fee, resistance came not from the owners but from the custodians, who saw the change as a threat to their income. Objections came from other quarters as well. In the 1770s the Emperor Joseph II moved his collection of paintings outside the Hofburg to the Upper Belvedere and introduced free admission. The curators, as we have already mentioned, protested, but so too did artists, on the curious grounds that the presence of the public disturbed 'the silent contemplation of the works of art'.

In Rome, matters were arranged in a democratic fashion. During the eighteenth century, there was no difficulty in seeing, for example, the paintings in the Quirinal Palace on prescribed days. In Spain, anyone could see the royal art treasures in the Escorial. On the other hand, the pictures belonging to the French monarchy remained inaccessible to the public until halfway through the eighteenth century, when, as a result of petitions that the Palace of Versailles should make some part of the huge collections generally available, about 100 paintings were provisionally hung in the Luxembourg Palace, in Paris, where the public could look at them on two days a week. The experiment was short-lived, however.

England had a particularly bad name for the secrecy and possessiveness of her collectors. As the German scholar and traveller, Winckelman, put it, after a visit to England in 1760, 'Those barbarians, the English, buy up everything and in their own country nobody sees it but themselves.' The accusation was not unfair. The wealthy English, who bought extensively in

Italy and other continental countries during the seventeenth
and eighteenth centuries, had no feeling at all that their collections might, as cultural assets, belong to the nation as a whole
and that it was irresponsible to prevent other people from
enjoying them. Some at least of the German courts took a much
more progressive view. The gallery at Dresden could be viewed
without difficulty from 1746 onwards. It was housed in a building outside the palace, which made public admission easy to organise; and at Salzdahlum, near Brunswick, there were
conducted tours, lasting two hours.

One should not be too hard on either the English collectors or
the eighteenth century. A wish to keep the public away from
one's treasures is not peculiarly English and, if the wealthy
eighteenth-century English collectors seemed particularly sel-
fish, this was to some extent because there was, compared with
other European countries, such a number of them and, perhaps
even more important, because a high proportion of the English
collections were not inherited. They belonged to the men who
had built them up from nothing, men with the desire to possess,
which, as Lord Clark has pointed out, is 'a biological function,
not unrelated to our physical appetites'.[4] It is, he continues,

> no accident that the great, greedy collectors, Augustus of
> Saxony, Catherine of Russia, Caylus, Vivant-Denon, not to
> mention more recent examples, were also great amorists.
> There is also some of the miser's instinct, which gives the
> works collected a kind of totemic value:
>
> > Good morning to the day and next, my gold
> > Open the shrine, that I may see my *Saint* . . .
>
> Mr Gulbenkian, when asked to show his collection, used to
> reply, 'Would I admit a stranger to my harem?' And at least
> two great collectors have assured me that, like Sardanapalus
> and his wives, they wished their collections to be burnt on
> their deaths. Nor is this attitude wholly unsympathetic.
> Great collections are often made by men who have held high
> office, and have, in consequence, few illusions about the
> nature of their fellow men, or women. Pictures become their
> only reliable friends.

On this theory, it was relatively easy for the Emperor Joseph
II to give the public access to his paintings, since they had been

largely gathered together by his ancestors, not by himself personally. But it was undoubtedly an act of great political wisdom. A French scholar, René Huyge, has pointed out[5] the significant fact that public museums and encyclopaedias appeared at the same time. Both were an expression of the eighteenth-century spirit of enlightenment which produced an enthusiasm for equality of opportunity in learning. In England, the publication of Chambers's *Cyclopaedia* was contemporary with the creation of the British Museum, and France put part of the royal collections on show in the Luxembourg at the same time as the *Encyclopédistes* published their programme. The theory behind these movements was a simple one, that collections which had hitherto been reserved for the pleasure and instruction of a few people should be made accessible to everybody. The practice was, unfortunately but perhaps inevitably, very different. When public museums, such as the British Museum, were established, they carried on the traditions of the private collections. They might belong to the state, or to a body of trustees, but they were as exclusive, élitist and, not infrequently, precious, as their predecessors. They met the needs of a very small section of the public.

Probably the most important fact about seventeenth- and eighteenth-century museums and art galleries is that they were run by autocrats, who asked for nobody's advice or suggestions as to how the collections should be presented or organised. Visitors were admitted as a privilege, not as a right, and consequently gratitude and admiration, not criticism, was required of them.

This attitude persisted long after the widespread establishment of public museums in the modern sense. The new museums may have been provided for the benefit of the public at large, and financed from public funds, but they were very much the creations of their directors, who took the decisions as to how the buildings were to be designed, what system of display was to be adopted, what material was to be shown and what excluded. Consumer research was altogether foreign to the way in which the heads of most nineteenth-century museums thought about their task. They measured their success by the number of people who came through the turnstiles. What the people thought about the museum, or whether they were

coming for the first or the last time was of no particular consequence. For them to have invited public comment on their museums would have been as unthinkable as for a Victorian vicar
to have handed out to his congregation questionnaire forms relating to his sermon and his conduct of the service.

When they were carrying out research into the published results of surveys of museum visitors, Stephen Borhegyi and Irene
Hanson, of the Milwaukee Public Museum, found nothing earlier than 1897.[6] After this, a book published in Leipzig,[7] there
was a long gap until 1928, when American museums began to
interest themselves seriously in classifying and investigating
their customers. Since the 1950s, such surveys have become
commonplace all over the world, but even so, only a small minority of museums appear to have commissioned them. In
London, the Science Museum, which is one of the most heavily
and regularly patronised of all the major museums, has never
troubled to discover in any methodical way what the public
thinks about the face it is offered.

Consequently, in attempting to discover what kind of impact
museums have had on their visitors, one is compelled to rely on
evidence which is in no way scientific. One searches for comments wherever they are to be found, realising that only the
exceptional person is ever likely to write down his feelings and
find a published outlet for them and that the great majority of
men, women, boys and girls who have ever entered a museum
or an art gallery have been interested or bored, stupefied or in-
vigorated, without anybody but themselves or their friends
knowing about it.

Yet, however imperfect and untypical it may be as evidence,
what these seventeenth-, eighteenth- and nineteenth-century
people took the trouble to record provides a useful guide to the
success or failure of the owners and organisers of the collections. *This*, we may say, was being aimed at; and *this* was the
effect on at least one person. To be able to read the results of a
visitor research survey carried out among visitors to the British
Museum in 1800 or to the Peabody Museum in 1850 would be a
remarkable pleasure, but one which, alas, we shall never have.
This being so, we must try to content ourselves with the kind of
material which follows.

I

ENTRY AS A PRIVILEGE

In 1784, William Hutton, a Birmingham bookseller, visited the British Museum. It had not been easy to obtain one of the rare and much sought-after entrance tickets, but eventually he came across a man who was willing to part with his for two shillings, and he was able to turn his thoughts to the pleasures ahead.

> Here [he was certain] I shall regale the mind for two hours upon striking objects; objects which ever change and ever please. I shall see what is no where else to be seen. The wonders of creation are deposited in this vast cabinet. Every country upon the globe has, perhaps, paid its richest tribute into this grand treasury. The sea has unlocked its stores. The internal parts of the earth have been robbed of their spoils. The most extraordinary productions of art find their way into this repository, and the long ages of antiquity have largely contributed to the store.[1]

What actually happened at 11 a.m. on Tuesday, 7 December, was far from pleasant.

> We assembled on the spot, about ten in number, all strangers to me, perhaps to each other. We began to move pretty fast, when I asked with some surprise, whether there were none to inform us what the curiosities were as we went on? A tall genteel young man, *in person*, who seemed to be our conductor, replied with some warmth, 'What! would you have me tell you everything in the Museum? How is it possible? Besides, are not the names written upon many of them?' I was much too humbled by this reply to utter another word. The company seemed influenced; they made haste, and were silent.

No voice was heard but in whispers. If a man pass two minutes in a room, in which are a thousand things to demand his
attention, he cannot find time to bestow on them a glance
each. When our leader opens the door of another apartment,
the silent language of that action is, *come along*.

If I see wonders which I do not understand, they are no
wonders to me. Should a piece of withered paper lie on the
floor, I should, without regard, shuffle it from under my feet.
But if I am told it is a letter written by Edward the Sixth, that
information sets a value upon the piece, it becomes a choice
morceau of antiquity, and I seize it with rapture. The history
must go together; if one is wanting, the other is of little value.
I considered myself in the midst of a rich entertainment, consisting of ten thousand rarities, but, like Tantalus, I could not
taste one. It grieved me to think how much I lost for want of a
little information. In about *thirty minutes* we finished our silent
journey through this princely mansion, which would well
have taken thirty days. I went out much about as wise as I
went in, but with this severe reflection, that for fear of losing
my chance, I had that morning abruptly torn myself away
from three gentlemen, with whom I was engaged in an interesting conversation, had lost my breakfast, got wet to the
skin, spent half-a-crown in coach hire, paid two shillings for a
ticket, been hackneyed through the rooms with violence, had
lost the little share of good humour I brought in, and came
away completely disappointed.[2]

The original rules and regulations of the British Museum seem
to have been expressly calculated to keep the general public out
and to make sure that the few who did eventually make the tour
got as little pleasure and profit from it as possible. When the
Museum was first opened, in 1759, the Trustees published a list
of 'Statutes and Rules relating to the inspection and use of the
British Museum'.[3] These laid down, among other things, that
'such studious and curious persons' as might wish to see the collections must first make a written application to the Porter, giving their occupation, name and address. They then had to call
at some later date for their tickets, which entitled them to a visit
the following day. This procedure was likely to take at least two
weeks, and the investigations into credentials could last as long
as several months.

Not more than ten tickets were to be issued for each hour of admittance and nobody was allowed to look at anything without being closely attended by a member of the staff. Each group had to march through all the departments, with a bell to ring them from one department to another. A maximum of three hours was allowed to see the whole museum – Hutton was rushed through exceptionally fast – and children below the age of ten were rigorously excluded.

The general public were admitted on Mondays, Tuesdays, Wednesdays and Thursdays. Fridays were reserved for select parties, which included students of the Royal Academy. The Statutes made it quite clear that the main users of the Museum were to be artists and men of letters. The admission of other people was considered to be 'popular but far less useful', and it was restricted to eight groups of not more than fifteen persons each during the course of a day.

Although it is certainly true that the infant British Museum saw as its main purpose the provision of facilities to allow artists and scholars to study, it is probable that the general public would have been better treated than it actually was if Parliament had not left the Museum so chronically short of money. The persistent refusal to enlarge the Parliamentary grant was the main reason for the staff shortage which made it necessary to hustle visitors through the galleries at such a ridiculous speed and to limit so drastically the number who could be admitted each day.

The effect of such short-sighted meanness on the part of the Government was to perpetuate the tradition which made admission to a museum a privilege and a favour, not a right, a tradition which should have been brought to an end by the establishment of public museums. It is a curious paradox that until the middle of the nineteenth century the people with the best chance of seeing the pictures and other works of art in private collections belonged to a class that was probably little interested in its opportunities – domestic servants. We have no record of any impression which the treasures kept in great houses may have made on the housemaids, footmen and majordomos who were in constant contact with them, but from the occasional visitors we do considerably better.

One of the finest private collections at the beginning of the seventeenth century was that brought together by the Earl of Arundel and kept at his house in London, near the Strand. The German artist, Joachim von Sandrart, was allowed to see it during his visit to England in 1627. He described 'the beautiful garden of that most famous lover of art, the Earl of Arundel' as being 'resplendent with the finest ancient statues of marble, of Greek and Roman workmanship.'[4] Among these he noticed 'some full-lengths, some busts only, with an almost innumerable quantity of heads and reliefs all in marble and very rare'.

It will be observed that Sandrart contents himself with very general comments. The statuary was 'the finest' and 'very rare' and there was an 'almost innumerable quantity' of it. It clearly made a strong total impression on him and he was pleased and flattered to have been admitted, but he leaves us with no information about any particular work which may have struck him as outstanding or remarkable, and to have criticised the arrangement in any way would have been a sign of ingratitude, if not of impertinence. The Earl was 'that most famous lover of art', and the excellence of his taste could be assumed.

As a connoisseur he stood alone, in the size and range of his collections and in the personal knowledge and enthusiasm which had brought them together. In addition to the statues and inscribed Greek marbles, which were brought to England at enormous expense, there was the gallery of paintings, in which Holbein[5] and the Venetian School were particularly strongly represented, and a remarkable library. The most distinguished visitor to Arundel House was undoubtedly King Charles I, who had been familiar with the collection since his teens. It was probably Lord Arundel's example which helped him to develop the love of art for which he afterwards became celebrated.[6]

But to have brought all these works of art from Italy, Germany, the Netherlands, Greece and the Middle East and set them one against another in Arundel House, for the instruction and pleasure of the Earl and his friends and visitors, was to transform them into something different from what they had been when they were originally created. The museum, an entirely European development, removes the picture or the statue from its context and compels us to see it as an abstract thing, a work of art. To analyse and describe an object in terms of this new concept, a work of art, demands a new attitude, special training and a specialised phraseology. Seventeenth-century collectors and connoisseurs were at the beginning of this process and it is consequently not surprising that even such professional visitors as Joachim von Sandrart seem at a loss for words.

The point has been very well made by André Malraux. 'A Romanesque crucifix', he reminds us,[7] 'was not regarded by its contemporaries as a work of sculpture, nor Cimabue's "Madonna" as a picture. Even Pheidias' "Pallas Athene" was not, primarily, a statue.' The effect of the museum was 'to divest works of art of their functions. It did away with the significance of Palladium, of Saint and Saviour; ruled out associations of sanctity, qualities of adornment and possession, of likeness or imagination.' In its original setting, a painting or a piece of sculpture contributes to a mood of relaxation, which makes contemplation possible. Put into a gallery, it has to compete with other works, in an atmosphere which is neutral, if not actually hostile. An art gallery, says Malraux, 'is as preposterous as would be a concert in which one listened to a programme of ill-assorted pieces following in unbroken succession'. In such a situation, our approach to art has grown steadily more intellectualised. If our emotions are crippled, we can only interpret through our brain.

This is true not only of art museums. A machine is transformed into a dead artefact once it is torn from its natural habitat and put on show in a building which neither looks, smells nor feels like a workshop or the factory where it had function and meaning. A stuffed elephant in a museum is a stuffed elephant in a museum, not an elephant. An illuminated codex loses most of its significance, but none of its beauty, once it is removed from the religious atmosphere of the monastery where it belonged. Only the person of exceptional imagination, knowledge and powers of detachment can restore to an object the associations and the qualities which the museum has taken away.

Collectors are essentially robbers and destroyers. It makes little difference whether the collector is Andrew Mellon or the Metropolitan Museum of Art. There is simply too much of everything, in too artificial a situation to make anything more than an intellectual response possible, although just oc-

casionally the extraordinary force of a work of art will allow it to
break loose from the gallery-bonds which hold it down. It is no
accident that museums have become temples of scholarship,
since their intellectual emphasis is so strong. But most visitors
to museums are not intellectuals, and this is the source of the
major problems which curators have been facing for many
years.

If one says that paintings and sculptures have a meaning and
a stimulus in their original location which is usually lost when
they are removed to a museum, this must not be taken to mean
that art was once a purely spiritual activity and has only recently become a trade. In seventeenth- and eighteenth-century
Rome artists were commissioned to produce what was in effect
wallpaper, paintings to cover the walls of a particular room in
symmetrical patterns. The painter often asked for and received
very specific instructions. In 1665, for instance, Guercino was
given a commission to paint an altarpiece for a monastery in
Sicily. He was supplied with the exact measurements of the picture and told that he was to show 'the Madonna del Carmine
with the Child in Her arms, St. Teresa receiving the habit from
the Virgin and the rules of the Order from the Child, St. Joseph
and St. John the Baptist; these figures must be shown entire
and life-size, and the top part of the picture must be beautified
with frolicking angels.'[8] Guercino wrote back to ask whether
the Madonna

> is to be clothed in red with a blue cloak following church cus-
> tom or whether she should be in a black habit with a white
> cloak. Should the rules of the Order which the Child is hand-
> ing to the Saint be in the form of a book or a scroll? In that
> case what words should be written on it to explain the
> mystery? Further, should St. Teresa go on the left or the
> right?

Information such as this is part of art-historians' stock-in-
trade. It is interesting, and probably worth knowing, but it
adds nothing to the painting's power to communicate and
serves mainly to divide scholars from non-scholars. The growth
of connoisseurship during the eighteenth and nineteenth centuries inevitably made ordinary people feel inferior when faced
with works of art. So long as a religious painting or statue or

monstrance remained in a church, it had no élitist associations. It belonged to everybody and had meaning for everybody. Once it was moved to an art gallery, a different set of values came into play. It had to be judged in its own right, as an artistic production, and that needed experience and a specialised vocabulary. Museums have a remarkable power of making the uneducated feel inferior.

In one city, however, Rome, the general public was able to at least see paintings, especially new paintings, with no trouble at all, even in the early seventeenth century. Well-to-do people came to Rome from other parts of Italy and from abroad in order to buy paintings, and dealers set up shop in order to do business with them. This development was by no means universally approved. 'It is serious, lamentable, indeed intolerable to everybody', declared the Accademia di S. Luca, 'to see works destined for the decoration of Sacred Temples or the splendour of noble palaces exhibited in shops or in the streets, like cheap goods for sale.'⁹ By 1700, there were four regular exhibitions a year in Rome, in March, July, August and December, in addition to occasional ones organised for a particular event or a particular artist. The climate of Rome gave the public access to pictures in a way which would not have been possible in London, Paris or Amsterdam, without causing serious damage to the paintings. They were hung outside churches and dealers' shops, ranged along the walls of cloisters and even propped up against tombs in cemeteries.

'All this', says Francis Haskell, 'was leading to a growing appreciation of pictures as pictures, rather than as exclusively the record of some higher truth; a body of connoisseurs was coming into being prepared to judge pictures on their aesthetic merits, and consequently the subject-matter of paintings was losing its old primaeval importance.'¹⁰ This attitude – the Fine Art attitude – which became generally apparent only in the eighteenth century, and which is regarded as normal today, does not deserve the wholehearted welcome that has been given to it by Western art historians. It is socially divisive to an extreme degree and creates an artificial, vicious and totally unnecessary barrier between goods prized for their function and goods prized for their intrinsic beauty.

It is instructive, in this connexion, to study Zoffany's *Tribuna of the Uffizi*, exhibited at the Royal Academy, London, in 1780. It shows the annual judging and selection of paintings and sculpture at the Uffizi Gallery in Florence. All the people shown in the painting are specialists of one kind or another; artists, anxious to get their works approved, shown and sold, experts qualified to pass judgment on the merit and value of each item, and dealers and prospective purchasers, whose principal aim was to keep in touch with the market and with those who supplied it. What the public eventually saw was the fruits of all this appraisal and merchandising. There was nothing secret about it. Art had a strongly commercial tradition in Italy. There was always plenty of it about and the artist was regarded, quite properly, unless, as was very unlikely, he happened to be a genius, as a slightly superior tradesman. One might go further and say that, until the late nineteenth century, the public attitude to art was healthier in Italy than in either America or North-West Europe. Once a Tintoretto had made the long, perilous and expensive journey from Italy to London or St Petersburg it had inevitably acquired a value and a mystique which it did not possess in its native land. Chinese porcelain underwent a similar transfiguration and beatification.

The situation in Italy was exceptional. What happened in England was more typical of developments in Europe as a whole. The first English exhibition of contemporary art took place in 1760, at a room in the Strand belonging to the Society of Arts. Admission was free in the mornings, but sixpence was charged for a catalogue. The exhibition lasted only a fortnight and in that time 6582 catalogues were sold. For most of the poorer visitors it must have been their first opportunity to see pictures of any quality, but their behaviour, or possibly their presence, was not pleasing to the Society, which decided that at the second exhibition, held in the following year, there should be no free admittance. The first experiment had shown, it was claimed, that the result of making no charge was that the room was 'crowded and incommoded by the intrusion of great numbers whose stations and education made them no proper judges of statuary or painting and who were made idle and tumultuous by the opportunity of a show.'[11]

It is quite possible that the more humble visitors became 'idle and tumultuous' because they found the atmosphere strange and the works of art baffling. Pandora's box had been opened and what it contained was mystifying and disappointing. This was a not uncommon situation. Many owners of private collections had come to the conclusion long before the exhibition at the Society of Arts that it was unwise to admit all and sundry, simply because many of the visitors were hopelessly out of place.

> They had endured humiliating interrogations to obtain admission to a place described to them as a land of wonders, and they discovered that they were aliens in it. Some people found an outlet in inappropriate and rambunctious behaviour. Without clues to the many strange things around them either in their own minds or in such explanations as were offered in private cabinets and galleries, people would rush around from one thing to another and hunt for meaning. They lacked in most cases not only a background of specific knowledge into which the new experiences could be fitted, but all general education of a literate kind.[12]

In the second exhibition of the Society of Artists of Great Britain, which took place in a new room at Spring Gardens, the shilling catalogue entitled the visitor to come as often as he liked. A young army officer took full advantage of this system and went to Spring Gardens every day for a week. His father asked him to describe some of the pictures, which included five by Reynolds, and he wrote back as follows:

> When I entered the room, I was at a loss where first to fix my eyes, seeing so glaring a sight; but as, Dear Sir, my turn is military, you'll excuse me not keeping to the order of the catalogue, which has served me as a ticket for six or seven days. Mr. Scott's piece of the taking of Quebec gave me great pleasure: the French ships on fire are finely expressed. Not far from this is another picture of a general on Horseback, very different from the many modern and little inferior to some of the greatest masters of the ancients. There is an officer of the Guards with a letter in his hand, ready to mount his horse with all that fire mixed with rage that war and the love of his country can give; in the background a view of a skirmish. These pieces by Mr. Reynolds give me great satisfaction. I hope that gentleman will oblige the world with a

print of them, which if he does he will have military sub-
scribers enough. By the same ingenious person is a nobleman
in his college robes, a very fine piece.[13]

It is difficult to say to what extent the lieutenant was a typical
visitor. He certainly had stamina and determination. Not many
people can have gone to see the pictures day after day, as he did.
His first reaction, it will be noticed, was one of bewilderment,
when confronted with 'so glaring a sight'. Very wisely, he decided to concentrate on the pictures that interested him and
these, with one exception, were all of military subjects. Phrases
such as 'gave me great pleasure' and 'finely expressed' suggest
that the choice of subject appealed to him and that the painter's
view of war and the military life coincided with his own. He
appears to be quite unconcerned with the artist's technique or
reputation and he judges it unnecessary to provide his father
with more than the barest details of each painting.

Twelve years later, Susan Burney visited Sir Ashton Lever's
natural history museum in London, at his home, Leicester
House. She described the collection in a letter to her sister,
Madame D'Arblay.

Saturday morning we spent extremely well at Sir Ashton
Lever's Museum. I wish I was a good Natural Historian, that
I might give you some idea of our entertainment in seeing
birds, beasts, shells, fossils, etc. but I can scarce remember a
dozen names of the thousand I heard that were new to me.
The birds of paradise, and the humming birds, were, I think,
among the most beautiful. There are several pelicans, fla-
mingos, peacocks (one quite white), a penguin. Among the
beasts a hippopotamus (sea horse) of an immense size, an
elephant, a tyger from the Tower, a Greenland bear and its
cub – a wolf – two or three leopards – a Otaheite[14] dog (a very
coarse ugly-looking creature) – a camelion – a young croco-
dile – a roomful of monkeys – one of them presents the company with an Italian song – another is reading a book (are
these alive perhaps?) – another the most horrid of all, is put
in the attitude of Venus de Medicis, and is scarce fit to be
looked at. Lizzards, bats, toads, frogs, scorpions and other
filthy things in abundance. There were a great many things
from Otaheite (probably from Captain Cook's voyage) – the

complete dress of a Chinese Mandarine, made of blue and brown sattin – of an African Prince. A suit of armor that they say belonged to Oliver Cromwell – the Dress worn in Charles 1st's time, etc. etc.

Lever's collection was in no sense scientific. It was an assembly of objects, mostly within the field of natural history, which had been brought back to England by travellers and explorers. Lever, who was a lively-minded eccentric with the money to indulge his whims, enjoyed the exoticism of it all, and found added pleasure in putting his stuffed animals into the absurd postures noted by Susan Burney. But what he created was a museum, not a sideshow at a fair. All the items were genuine, in marked contrast to the sort of nonsense castigated earlier in the century in *The Tatler*.[15] In the village of Chelsea, there was, it appears, a coffee-house run by a certain Mr Salter. 'When I came into the Coffee-house,' the story goes, 'I had not time to salute the Company, before my Eye was diverted by ten thousand Gimcracks round the Room, and on the Cieling'. Mr Salter was an engaging man, with a Quixotic imagination that graded up and transformed his 'ten thousand Gimcracks', turning very ordinary articles into great rarities. 'He shews you a Straw-Hat, which I know to be made within three miles of Bedford; and tells you *it is* Pontius Pilate's Wife's Chambermaid's Sister's Hat.'

Sir Hans Sloane's collections of natural history and ethnography were of a very different order. They contained specimens of plants, animals, birds, fossils, minerals, as well as antiquities, works of art, coins, books and ethnographical material; and they were visited and studied by scientifically-minded men from all over Europe. After his death, they were bequeathed to the nation, 'to the manifestation of the glory of God, the confutation of atheism and its consequences, the use and improvement of physic, and other arts and sciences, and benefit of mankind', and they became the core of the new British Museum. Scholars undoubtedly rated Sir Hans Sloane's museum higher than that of Sir Ashton Lever, but whether the general public would have taken the same view, had it been equally free to visit both, is open to doubt.

In 1748, when Sloane was an old man, his museum was

visited by the Prince and Princess of Wales. We have a detailed account of what they saw and what they thought of it all.[16]

Dr. Mortimer, secretary to the Royal Society, conducted their Royal Highnesses into the room where Sir Hans was sitting, being antient and infirm. The Prince took a chair and sat down by the good old gentleman some time, when he expressed the great esteem and value he had for him personally, and how much the learned world was obliged to him for his having collected such a vast library of curious books, and such immense treasures of the valuable and instructive productions of nature and art. Sir Hans's house forms a square of above 100 feet each side, including a court; and three front-rooms had tables set along the middle, which were spread over with drawers fitted with all sorts of precious stones in their natural beds, or state as they are found in the earth, except the first, that contained stones formed in animals, which are so many diseases of the creature that bears them; as the most beautiful pearls, which are but warts in the shell fioh; the *bezoars*, concretions in the stomach, and stones generated in the kidneys and bladder, of which man woefully knows the effects; but the earth in her bosom generates the verdant *emerald*, the purple *amethist*, the golden *topaz*, the azure *saphire*, the crimson *garnet*, the scarlet *ruby*, the brilliant *diamond*, the glowing *opal*, and all the painted varieties that *Flora* herself might wish to be deck'd with; here the most magnificent vessels of cornelian, onyx, sardonyx and jasper, delighted the eye, and raised the mind to praise the great creator of all things.

When their Royal Highnesses had view'd one room, and went into another, the scene was shifted, for, when they returned, the same tables were covered for a second course with all sorts of *jewels*, polish'd and set after the modern fashion, or with *gems* carv'd or engraved; the stately and instructive remains of antiquity; for the third course the tables were spread with *gold* and *silver ores*, with the most precious and remarkable ornaments used in the *habits* of men, from *Siberia* to the Cape of *Good Hope*, from *Japan* to *Peru*; and with both antient and modern *coins* and *medals* in gold and silver, the lasting monuments of historical facts; as those of a *Prusias*, king of *Bithynia*, who betray'd his allies; of an *Alexander*,

who, mad with ambition, over-run and invaded his neighbours; of a *Caesar*, who inslaved his country to satisfy his own
pride; of a *Titus*, the delight of mankind; of a Pope *Gregory*
XIII, recording on a silver medal his blind zeal for *religion*, in
perpetuating thereon the *massacre* of the *protestants* in *France*;
as did *Charles* IX, the then reigning king in that country; here
may be seen the coins of a *king* of *England*, crown'd at *Paris*; a
medal representing *France* and *Spain*, striving which should
first pay their obeissance to *Britannia*; others shewing the effect of popular rage, when overmuch oppressed by their
superiors; as in the case of the *De Witts* in *Holland*; the happy
deliverance of *Britain*, by the arrival of King *William*; the
glorious exploits of a Duke of *Marlborough*, and the happy
arrival of the present illustrious *royal family* amongst us.

The gallery, 120 feet in length, presented a most surprising
prospect; the most beautiful *corals, crystals,* and figured
stones; the most brilliant *butterflies,* and other insects, *shells*
painted with as great variety as the precious stones, and fea-
thers of *birds* vying with gems; here the remains of the *Antedi-
luvian* world excited the awful idea of that great catastrophe,
so many evident testimonies of the truth of *Moses*'s history;
the variety of animals shews us great beauty of all parts of the
creation.

Then a noble vista presented itself thro' several rooms
filled with books, among these many hundred volumes of
dry'd plants; a room full of choice and valuable manuscripts;
the noble present sent by the present *French* king to Sir *Hans*,
of his collections of paintings, medals, statues, palaces, &c in
25 large atlas volumes; besides other things too many to men-
tion here.

Below-stairs some rooms are filled with the curious and
venerable antiquities of *Egypt, Greece, Hetruria, Rome, Britain,*
and even *America*; others with large animals preserved in the
skin; the great *saloon* lined on every side with bottles filled
with spirits, containing various animals. The halls are
adorned with the horns of divers creatures, as the
double-horn'd *Rhinoceros* of *Africa*, the fossil deer's horns from
Ireland nine feet wide; and with weapons of different countries, among which it appears that the *Mayalese*, and not our
most *Christian* neighbours the *French*, had the honour of

inventing that butcherly weapon the *bayonet*. Fifty volumes in folio would scarce suffice to contain a detail of his immense museum, consisting of above 200,000 articles.

Their *royal highnesses* were not wanting in expressing their satisfaction and pleasure, at seeing a collection, which surpass'd all the notions or ideas they had form'd from even the most favourable accounts of it. The Prince, on this occasion shew'd his great reading and most happy memory; for in such a multiplicity, such a variety of the productions of nature and art, upon any thing being shewn him he had not seen before, he was ready in recollecting where he had read of it; and upon viewing the ancient and modern *medals*, he made so many judicious remarks, that he appear'd to be a perfect master of *history* and *chronology*; he express'd the great pleasure it gave him to see so magnificent a collection in *England*, esteeming it an ornament to the nation; and expressed his sentiments how much it must conduce to the benefit of learning, and how great an honour will redound to *Britain*, to have it established for publick use to the latest posterity.

Not all art is meant to be looked at in a spirit of reverence, a truth which often escapes art historians. To stand quietly and as near as possible invisibly among, say, the large collection of Picassos at the Museum of Modern Art in New York, and to listen to the earnest conversations which surround even the painter's most frolicsome and light-hearted canvases is to realise the leaden feet on which criticism and scholarship can make their way. If Greece, Rome, the Middle Ages and the Renaissance had been as overwhelmingly serious-minded as the scholars and antiquarians of the eighteenth and nineteenth centuries made them out to be, life in those periods would indeed have been hard to bear.

One of the most powerful formative influences on eighteenth-century taste was the Society of Dilettanti.[17] It was founded in 1732, the majority of the original members being wealthy young men who had recently returned from their Grand Tour of the Continent and consequently felt themselves equipped to be the arbiters of culture in their own country. Many of them subsequently went on to become important figures in politics, the court, the church, commerce or the army.

The Society pioneered the serious study of classical archaeology, mainly through the support it gave to James Stuart
and Nicholas Revett, whose splendidly illustrated book, *The
Antiquities of Athens*, was published in 1762.[18] It was written for
an educated public and, in the view of the Society's historian,
'revealed the important place in the history of art which the
existing remains of Greek sculpture and architecture still have a
right to hold'.[19]

Stuart and Revett described and drew classical antiquities.
Another member of the Society of Dilettanti, Charles Townley,
devoted most of his energy ai ɪ much of his money to buying
such antiquities and bringing them back to England. He lived
in Rome between 1765 and 1772 and helped to promote British
excavations there.[20] He bought many of the finest discoveries –
sculpture, bronzes, vases, coins and jewels – for his own collection, which he installed in a gallery at Park Street, Westminster, when he returned from Italy. He steadily added to his
collection and his house became the centre of a circle of people
with artistic interests, including many members of the Society
of Dilettanti. A group of them are shown with Townley in his
gallery in the famous painting by Zoffany. The picture conveys
very well the important fact that during the eighteenth century
an interest in art and antiquities was essentially an activity for
the leisured and the well-to-do. These were the people who
formed the canons of taste, decided what was worth collecting
and what was not, created the private galleries. Broadly speaking, the people who were invited to their dinner-parties were
also those who were always welcome as visitors to their galleries
and museums. It was a closed circle, within which the conversation about works of art was almost as important as the works
of art themselves. One senses this from contemporary paintings
of the interiors of private museums, where the groupings, attitudes and clothes of the visitors are of great significance. There
is a seventeenth-century picture by Ternier, now in the Kunsthistorisches Museum, Vienna, which shows the Archduke
Leopold Wilhelm of Hapsburg viewing paintings in his palace
in Brussels. What is shown in Ternier's picture is a storeroom,
rather than an exhibition gallery, from which items were taken
from time to time to grace the more important rooms in the
palace. Artists and other favoured people who were given entry

to the storeroom would come to know the pictures very well and, having got their bearings as a result of repeated visits, they would be able to devote their full attention to a particular painting and to cut out the visual commotion which would confuse the casual visitor, and which is the first thing that strikes anyone looking at Ternier's painting today. To anyone used to twentieth-century art galleries, the Archduke's collection gives the impression of utter chaos, but it would not necessarily have seemed like that at the time.

A clue to the way in which a connoisseur would first absorb the whole of what was presented to him and then select something which particularly appealed to him is given in an account of a visit paid to the collection of the Elector, Carl Theodor, in Mannheim in 1777.

> Here I stand exposed to the most wonderful impressions in a square and roomy hall with the most glorious statues of antiquity . . . a forest of statues. . . . After I had submitted for a time to the effect of this irresistible mass, I turned to those figures which attracted me most, and who can deny that the *Apollo Belvedere*, through its moderated immensity, his slender build and free movement, his victor's look, is beyond all the rest, and also victor over our feelings.[21]

A modern comparison might be to the sub-editor's office on a newspaper or to a large telephone switchboard, where the general noise is, to the outside observer, appalling, but creates no problems for those who are used to it. The journalist, like the telephonist, gradually learns to work and concentrate with bedlam all around him.

The Archduke certainly took a pleasure in discovering what connoisseurs had to say about his pictures. What in modern terms would be called the feedback of the people who came to see them constituted a great deal of the point of owning the collection. The visitors would almost certainly not publish their thoughts, but they would have thought it strange, ungrateful and discourteous not to utter them.

A similar situation can be deduced from the 1699 engraving,[22] by an anonymous artist, of one of the galleries in the Louvre. He again is showing us a storeroom, where the pictures are crammed together. The subjects are taken from the Bible, from history and from classical mythology, and there are a number of portraits. Each would have been an interpretation of something with which the courtiers and their friends shown in the picture would have been very familiar. Conversation about them would have been about nuances of feeling and points of style. The paintings formed part of the sub-culture and the pattern of life which all those walking round the gallery shared, and which a clerk, a washerwoman or a mechanic very obviously did not share.

Museums which were not devoted to the arts were in a different situation. There was no agreed taste relating to stuffed birds, no connoisseurship of Pacific island weapons or costumes. The non-art museums therefore rested on foundations which were, at least potentially, more democratic.

It is necessary to remember that most private collections, whatever the contents, were not arranged in a way which made it possible for more than a few people to see them at any one time. They were usually in the home of the owner and, however friendly and willing to welcome strangers he might be, it made no sense to have the rooms thronged with people who could see nothing. Once the principle of the public museum was accepted, the design of buildings and rooms capable of dealing with large numbers of people followed as a natural consequence. Even then, however, the material on display was usually far too crowded for anything approaching easy viewing. The wealthy private collectors lined the walls of their galleries with pictures from floor to ceiling, and crammed exhibition cases with objects, simply in order to get everything in.

One has to distinguish between, on the one hand, the wish of private collectors to exclude visitors who were culturally unsuitable – this applied especially to art galleries – and on the other the need to keep the numbers and behaviour of visitors under control. The difference between the two is well illustrated by a comparison of the aims and methods of Sir Ashton Lever, whose museum has already been referred to, and of Dr Richard Mead – both rich, enterprising and unquestionably public-spirited.

Sir Ashton was a country gentleman, born in 1729 and educated at Oxford. His house, Alkrington Hall, near Manchester, was well away from any of the fashionable centres. As a young man, he collected live birds, and by 1760 he was said to have the best aviary in Britain. He then broadened out into shells, fossils, ethnographical material and curiosities of all kinds. By 1774 the collection, which was much visited, had grown to such a size that life at Alkrington Hall had become somewhat difficult and Sir Ashton transferred his collection to London, where he opened a museum for the general public. He charged for admission, in order to cover his costs and to reduce the number of visitors. This policy was based on his experiences at Alkrington, where he had been driven to desperation and to putting this notice in the newspapers:[23]

> This is to inform the Publick that being tired out with the insolence of the common People, who I have indulged with a sight of my museum, I am now come to the resolution of refusing admittance to the lower class except they come provided with a ticket from some Gentleman or Lady of my acquaintance. And I hereby authorise every friend of mine to give a ticket to any orderly Man to bring in eleven Persons besides himself, whose behaviour he must be answerable for, according to the directions he will receive before they are admitted. They will not be admitted during the time of Gentlemen and Ladies being in the Museum. If it happens to be inconvenient when they bring their ticket, they must submit to go back and come again some other day, admittance in the morning *only* from eight o'clock till twelve.

What exactly did Sir Ashton mean by 'the insolence of the common People'? In what way was their behaviour so objectionable? It cannot have been because the museum seemed to threaten or diminish them. Birds, monkeys, beads and grass skirts can hardly have had this effect, even in the eighteenth century. There are probably two explanations, apart from the simple fact of ignorance. The first is that, having gained entrance to Alkrington Hall, the common people intended to use the opportunity in order to make clear that Jack was as good as his master, and the second that the exhibits Sir Ashton offered them reminded them of attractions at fairs – bears, two-headed calves, fat women, and so on. A fair was a recognised occasion for running a little wild, and the tradition spilled over on to Alkrington Hall. Whether they did any actual damage to the exhibits we are not told; but they were all too clearly a serious disappointment to Sir Ashton.

Dr Mead was one of the best known and most successful physicians in Europe in the 1740s. He spent a large part of his income buying pictures and bronzes. His gallery, at his house in Great Ormond Street, covered a wide range. There were paintings by, for example, Van Dyck, Rembrandt, Franz Hals, Rubens, Canaletto, Holbein, and Claude Watteau, who suffered from tuberculosis, was his patient and owed a great deal to his support as a patron. Mead was an extremely hospitable man. His friend and colleague, Dr Maty, said that

> no foreigner of any learning, taste or even curiosity, could ever come to England without being introduced to Dr. Mead; as it would have been a matter of reproach to have returned without seeing him. On these occasions, his table was always open; where, what seldom happens, the magnificence of Princes was united with the pleasure of Philosophers.[24]

Mead was unusually generous in allowing students to copy his pictures every morning, without any fee, at a time when the possibility at other collections in private houses was usually limited to a quick tour in exchange for a large tip to the servant or caretaker.[25] There is no evidence, however, that he even considered admitting the public at large, fee or no fee. He would have thought such a step both pointless and ridiculous.

We are speaking of a time when a high proportion of people in all the European countries could neither read nor write. Some of the visitors to Sir Ashton Lever's house may well have been totally illiterate and unable to read the labels or notices provided for their guidance. It would have been absurd, given the social stratification of the period and the obvious differences in dress, speech and manners which marked one class off from another, to have expected the educated and the uneducated to mingle easily or happily in the same room. The best that could reasonably be hoped for was that the demarcation line between potential and out-of-the-question museum visitors might be pushed downwards far enough to include what would nowadays be termed the lower middle class, shopkeepers, clerks, minor Civil Servants, with possibly a sprinkling of more aspiring and respectable artisans. Such people might not have a great deal of knowledge of the contents of the museum, private or public, but they would be literate and they could be trusted to behave themselves.

Evidence is sadly lacking on the point before the nineteenth century, but it seems very probable that during the seventeenth and eighteenth centuries those private collectors who either opened their collections 'to the public' or who bequeathed them to a city 'for the benefit of the public' had a restricted public in mind. It is not, of course, necessary to officially exclude certain categories of people in order to keep them away. Once people realise, possibly after a first visit, that a place is not for them, they can usually be depended on to stay outside. Difficulties are likely to arise only when people go expecting one thing and find something quite different. Disappointment is a potent source of trouble in any field.

Why, we can usefully ask, should anybody, even the educated, have wanted to visit a museum before the nineteenth century made this a normal activity? The question is worth putting in this form, because a number of very learned and cultured people – Dr Johnson is an outstanding example – never, so far as we know, crossed the threshold of a museum of any kind.

Without attempting any order of priority, we can suggest these possible reasons:

(*a*)   To study, to advance oneself in one's profession;
(*b*)   To help to educate oneself;
(*c*)   Curiosity, to widen one's horizons, for the pleasure of seeing something new;
(*d*)   To meet people with the same cultivated tastes as oneself;
(*e*)   For snobbish reasons, to rub shoulders with people of superior knowledge, taste or social status;
(*f*)   In order to say one has been;
(*g*)   For political reasons, to prove that the nation's cultural assets belong to the people as a whole.

The eighteenth century met the requirements of (*a*), (*c*), (*d*) and (*f*) very well, at least in the capital cities, (*e*) passably and (*b*) badly. Point (*g*) was becoming of considerable importance in Paris by the 1770s, as resentment grew against the concentration of wealth in the hands of the monarchy and the court, but it was showing itself in England and elsewhere in western Europe in another and less directly political form, the gradual shift in political and cultural power from a landed and mainly aristocratic group to a new class, whose money came from colonisation, foreign trade and manufacturing. The arts found a new type of patron and the ideal of a permanent canon of taste was abandoned in favour of fashion. The new middle-class patronage produced pictures that were, in John Steegman's excellent phrase, 'easy to read' and painters 'who could satisfy most simply, and with least effort to the beholder, those feelings that everybody must at some time experience.'[26] Art of this type, with its emphasis on the subject and the story, made a much stronger appeal to women of all classes, was more easily approached by the mass of the people, and exhibitions of it could be enjoyed by a much wider range of visitors. In this sense, the task of those whose business it was to build and organise art museums became easier as the nineteenth century went on, because, in all European countries, the supply of the new democratic art became more plentiful with each decade. At the same time, the belief grew that the business of education was with facts and morality, not with sensibility, and this in turn greatly influenced the way in which museum collections were organised and presented.

An example of this was the rearrangement of the picture collection of the Austrian Imperial House, when it was transferred to the Belvedere in 1781. In their former home, the Stallburg, the pictures were assembled to make a continuous wall-covering, cut, where necessary, to fit round the frames of the doors. The designer for the new museum, von Mecheln, aimed at a system comparable to a library, which would be 'educative' rather than 'enjoyable'. The pictures were put in rows, instead of as a tapestry, and small sculptures were regimented in cases. There was a division between artists from the north of Europe and artists from the south. The new scheme was praised by those who were glad to see order instead of confusion and attacked by those who found the machine-like regularity offensive to anyone possessing taste and sensitivity. Von Rittershausen said bluntly that 'the purpose of a gallery is not to offer historical knowledge but to develop taste and to awaken the noblest instincts of the heart'. If he could have looked ahead into the nineteenth century, he would have realised that he was fighting a losing battle. Facts were beginning to push out sensitivity, at least in the public museums. The day of the art historians was dawning, and nowhere more strongly and more clearly than in the German-speaking world.

But the old, early eighteenth-century world continued a long time in private houses. In the 1830s, a German art expert, G. F. Waagen, made an extensive tour of collections in Britain. He visited, among many others, Lord Cowper's collection of pictures at Panshanger and found nearly everything very much to his satisfaction.

The glowing summer's sun had heated me exceedingly, but I was soon revived by the refreshing coolness of these fine apartments, in which the pictures are arranged with much taste. The drawing-room, especially, is one of those apartments which not only give great pleasure by their size, the convenience and elegance of the furniture, but likewise afford the most elevated gratification of the mind, by works of art of the noblest kind. This splendid apartment receives light from three lanterns, and large windows at one of the ends: and the paintings of the Italian school are very well relieved by the purple silk hangings. I cannot refrain from again praising the refined taste of the English, who adorn their rooms, which are in daily use, in this manner, and thus experience, often from their youth, the silent and the slow, but sure, influence of works of art.

I passed here six happy hours in quiet solitude. The solemn silence was interrupted only by the humming of innumerable bees, which fluttered round the flowering plants which, in the greatest luxuriance, adorn the windows. It is only when so left to oneself, that by degrees, penetrating into the spirit of works of art, one can discover all their peculiar beauties. But when, as often happens in England, and, as I shall doubtless again experience, an impatient housekeeper rattles with her keys, one cannot of course be in the proper frame of mind, but must look at everything superficially, and with internal vexation.[27]

With this temperament, Waagen must have suffered terrible frustrations in public art galleries, where there were distractions worse than a key-rattling housekeeper. Of some aspects of his English tour he was, however, a severe critic. At Corsham, in Wiltshire, for instance, matters were not at all to his liking. The collection here, he found,

> very naturally indicates the taste of the time in which it was formed, and the pictures of the later Italian schools accordingly predominate. But it likewise contains a considerable number of excellent works of the better periods of the several schools, the value of which is probably not recognised as it should be, in consequence of the very bad condition in which they are. This condition is caused by that destructive enemy to pictures, the damp; and it may be confidently predicted that all the pictures will be totally ruined in a few years, unless they are soon removed from Corsham House.[28]

The paintings are still there, restored, cleaned and, nowadays, dry and warm.

2

ENTRY AS A RIGHT

The pattern of museum growth in America has been exactly the opposite of what took place in Europe. In Germany, Austria, France, England and the other European countries, the private collections came first and public museums developed from them. In America, public museums were in being many years before the great private collections began to be formed. It is true that during the present century many of the private collections have either been bequeathed to existing museums or transformed into public institutions, so reproducing a process which had been in evidence more than a century before in Europe; but by then the American idea of a museum established for the benefit of the whole community had struck deep roots.

The Charleston Museum, South Carolina, is usually reckoned to be the oldest in America,[1] but the date claimed for its foundation, 1773, has to be interpreted with some discretion, since, although plans were made in that year, the museum itself did not come into being until rather later. The initiative came from the Charleston Library Society, which had come into being in 1748. The Society collected, and lent out, scientific instruments as well as books, and a museum was a logical development of its activities.

The Society set out its plans and appealed for gifts of suitable exhibits in an advertisement published in the South Carolina newspaper during March and April, 1773. This read:

> Taking into their Consideration the many Advantages and great Credit that would result to this Province, from a full and accurate Natural History of the same, and being desir-

ous to promote so useful a Design, have appointed a Committee of their number to collect and prepare Materials for that Purpose.

That this may be done in the most complete and extensive Manner, they do now invite every Gentleman who wishes well to the undertaking, especially those who reside in the Country, to co-operate with them in the Advancement of this Plan. For this Purpose, the Society would Request such Gentlemen to procure and send to them, all the natural Productions, either Animal, Vegetable or Mineral, that can be had in their several Bounds, with Accounts of the various Soils, Rivers, Waters, Springs, etc. and the most remarkable Appearance of the different Parts of the Country.

Of the Animal Tribe, they would wish to have every Species, whether Terrestrial or Aquatic, viz Quadrupedes, Birds, Fishes, Reptiles, Insects, Worms, etc. with the best Accounts of their Customs and natural Habitudes.

Of Vegetables, they will thankfully receive every Kind, from the loftiest tree in the Forest, to the smallest Plant of the Fields. A complete Specimen of any Tree or Plant, will be two small Branches of each, one having the Flower in full Blossom, and the other the ripe Fruit. At the same Time the Society beg to be furnished with the best Accounts that can be given of the Uses and Virtues, either in Agriculture, Commerce, or Medicine, of which such Tree or Plant is possessed, the Soil in which it most commonly grows, the Season in which it flowers, and when it bears its Fruit.

They would be glad to be furnished also with Specimens of all the various Fossils, Minerals, and Ores, the different Soils, Earths, Clays, Marles, Stones, Sands, Shells, etc., the Productions of this Province, with the best Accounts of their several Natures, Qualities, Situations and Uses.

Co-operation of this kind was not intended to be a burden to anyone who helped the Society. 'Any Expence that may be incurred by forwarding Letters of Intelligence, Specimens etc. to Town', the advertisement concluded, 'the Society will chearfully repay'.

What eventually emerged within a few years was 'an extensive collection of Beasts, Birds, Reptiles, Fishes, Warlike Arms,

Dresses, and other Curiosities', by no means all relating to South Carolina. There were, for instance, a 'Head of a New Zealand Chief', an Egyptian mummy, the bones of an ostrich, a duck-billed platypus and 'Shoes of the Chinese Ladies, 4 inches long'. The collection was 'elegantly arranged in glass cases, open every day from 9 o'clock, and brilliantly illuminated every evening, with occasionally a Band of Music'. Admittance cost 25 cents, with children half price. A season ticket could be obtained for one dollar.

The Society's collections suffered greatly from a fire in 1778, and were moved to the State House in 1785. The museum was transferred to the newly established Literary and Philosophical Society of South Carolina in 1814. During the next forty years a number of private natural history collections were acquired, by donation or purchase, and a close link was established with the College of Charleston. In 1857 *Harper's New Monthly Magazine*[2] described it as 'one of the best museums in the United States, second perhaps to none'. After a period of decay, it was revived in 1907 by being taken over by the city council, and since then it has developed into a large and active public museum of the modern type.

The stages through which the Charleston Museum has passed during the two centuries of its history are typical of the way in which many public museums developed in the United States, always intended to benefit the public but having to adapt themselves to new financial situations and to new concepts of what a museum was for.

Peale's Museum in Philadelphia,[3] opened in 1782, resulted from the efforts of one man, not of a committee, but it was never regarded as a private collection. It had its origin in a collection of about forty portraits of some of his fellow officers during the American War of Independence, which Charles Wilson Peale painted during the campaign. These were first displayed in his own house, but by 1782 they had become so popular that Peale decided to build a new gallery, adjoining his house, to accommodate them. It had overhead lighting, the first gallery in the United States to be so designed.

The gallery was advertised in the press as being for 'the reception and entertainment of all lovers of the fine arts', and it attracted what Peale had hoped for, more visitors and more

commissions. It would probably not have developed any
further, however, if Peale had not been asked, in 1784, by a
German scholar to send him some drawings of what were described as 'mammoth bones'. While he had the bones in his
possession, Peale put them on exhibition in his gallery and was
surprised and pleased to discover that the number of visitors
considerably increased as a result. His brother-in-law, Colonel
Nathaniel Ramsey, thought there was nothing remarkable
about this. 'Doubtless', he said, 'there are many men like
myself who would prefer seeing such articles of curiosity than
any paintings whatever. It would be little trouble to keep them,
and the public would be gratified at the sight, at such time as
they came to see the paintings.'[4]

Peale's interests went in other directions for a couple of years,
but in 1786 he turned his full attention to the idea of a museum
and, having made up his mind that the idea had possibilities, he
advertised his new project in terms which would have seemed a
little strange on the other side of the Atlantic.

> Mr. Peale, ever desirous to please and entertain the public,
> will make a part of his house a repository for Natural Curi-
> osities – The Public he hopes will thereby be gratified in the
> sight of many of the Wonderful Works of Nature which are
> now closeted but seldom seen. The several articles will be
> classed and arranged according to their several species, and
> for greater ease to the Curious, on each piece will be
> inscribed the place from which it came, and the name of the
> Donor, unless forbid, with such further information as may
> be necessary.[5]

Visitors to the new and expanded collection had to pay an
admission fee of a shilling or a dollar for a season ticket lasting a
year. They were provided, among other things, with the results
of Peale's experiments with taxidermy. He put up warning
notices, saying 'Do not touch the birds, they are covered with
arsenic Poison', but they were often ignored and the visitors
concerned got more than they bargained for. An interesting
new development, which Peale pioneered, was to arrange the
birds and animals in habitat groups, with, for example, a 'flock
of wild Ducks belonging to this river, ducks and Drakes which I
have disposed in various attitudes on artificial ponds. Some

birds and beasts on trees, and some birds suspended as flying.'6

There was a grotto, with imitation rock, for the reptiles and fishes, with mirrors used to represent water.

Peale had a first-class sense of public relations. He was certainly one of the first, and quite possibly the first, to realise that benefactors to an institution obtained enormous satisfaction from seeing their generosity recorded in print. To do this, Peale resorted to making announcements in the local press. The following is typical:

> The horn and part of the tail of an American Horn Snake, presented by Miss Araminta Alexander, of Maryland.

> An American Pelican, entire and in good preservation, killed on the Chester River, Maryland, and presented by Colonel Tilghman.

> Two full-grown American Panthers, and a porcupine, presented by Captain Ferguson.

> An Albatros from the Cape of Good Hope, one of the largest of the feathered tribe, the wings extended measure 11 feet.

> A Jackall and Mangouste, both alive, from China. The last three presented by Captain Bell.

Peale's tastes were exceedingly catholic. Among the hundreds of items added to his collection between 1790 and 1792 were a chicken with four legs and four wings, an 80-pound turnip, the trigger-finger of a convicted murderer, and a tiny piece of wood from the Coronation chair in Westminster Abbey. The success of the appeal for new exhibits proved something of an embarrassment and Peale realised that his museum, if it were to survive, would have to be transformed into something much more like a public institution. He accordingly informed 'the Citizens of the United States of America', through a press advertisement,7 of his new plan 'to enable him to raise this tender plant, until it shall grow into full maturity and become a National Museum'. The idea was to set up a Board of Visitors, made up of 'gentlemen whose regard for science is well known', who would supervise the arrangement and growth of the Museum, attract money towards it and make sure that it had staff of the required quality. This was achieved, and what had begun as an accident grew within a short time into a museum of impressive size and respectable scientific standards, although ultimately it failed to survive as an independent concern.

Another early American museum of a similar type, although with a smaller emphasis on natural history, was that established in 1799 by the East India Marine Society at Salem.[8] The collections were formed of material brought back from all over the world by sea-captains. By 1804 the museum had outgrown its space and was installed in new premises. Twenty years later, in 1824, it moved again, this time to the newly-built East India Marine Hall. Entry was free until 1827, but, even with a charge, the Society found the burden impossible to bear and in 1866 the collections were bought by the Essex Institute, and added to its own to form a new museum, with money given by George Peabody. The Peabody Museum still remains and prospers.

In 1826, the Salem Museum was visited by an Italian, Giacomo Constantino Beltrami, who declared, with flattering exaggeration, that it was, beyond argument, the finest in the world. Beltrami celebrated its treasures and its excellence in Latin verse, a form of tribute which few museums have received.

> Siste Viator! Siste, mirare! Est Orbis in Urbe,
> Et praebet pulchrum cuncta miranda Salem.
> Obstupui, hic Superum, hic hominum, prodigia vidi,
> Pontus, Magna Parens, Ignis et Ipse favent.
> O America! O felix tellus, populusque beatus!
> Quam nobis tollunt dant tibi fata vicem.

A more conventional kind of comment came in the following year from the English traveller, James Silk Buckingham.
'I made several visits to the Museum,' he wrote, 'and was, on each occasion, abundantly gratified. The articles are well arranged, and kept in excellent order, and there is never so great a crowd of visitors as to prevent the careful and uninterrupted examination of any article at leisure.'[9] With its 'singular mixture and variety of curiosities', it could not, in Buckingham's opinion, fail 'to furnish abundant information and amusement to visitors of all classes, from the venerable navigator and hydrographer to the holiday pupil, as there is as much to entertain as to inform.'

Caroline Howard King was just such a 'holiday pupil'. Recalling the visits she paid to the Museum as a child in the 1830s, she wrote:

As far back as I can remember the Museum had a mysterious attraction for me and indeed it was an experience for an imaginative child to step from the prosaic streets of a New England town into that atmosphere redolent with the perfumes from the east, warm and fragrant and silent, with a touch of the dear old Arabian Nights about it. From the moment I set foot in that beautiful old hall, and greeted and was greeted by the solemn group of Orientals who, draped in eastern stuffs and camel's hair shawls, stood opposite the entrance, until the hours of closing came, and Captain Saul went through his never failing ceremony of presenting me with a slip of sandal wood cut from a huge log that stood near the door, or a sweet smelling Tonquin Bean, the hours were full of enchantment, and I think I came as near fairy-land as one ever can in this workaday world.

And that circle of sitting and standing figures, who were placed in the centre of the hall in those days, became real friends of mine. Three of them were life-sized likenesses of East Indian merchants, in their own dresses, presented to different sea captains by the originals, or perhaps sent to the Museum as gifts. I never heard their exact history, but I came to know their dark faces well, and Mr. Blue Gown, and Mr. Camel's Hair Scarf and Mr. Queer Cap, each had his own pleasant individuality and must be greeted whenever I went to the Museum. And indeed in those days the Spice Islands seemed to lie very near our Coast.[10]

Charleston, the Peale Museum and Salem grew in what could be called the typical early museum way. The collections piled up in a completely disorderly, unplanned fashion yet, as the memories of Caroline Howard King testify, this old-fashioned chaos had a strong appeal for children and other unsophisticated people, for whom a museum was, more than anything else, a chamber of wonders, a romantic place which scientific arrangement could and did only spoil.

The enthusiastic early nineteenth century collector was only in rare instances an orderly, systematic person. The more he acquired, the better pleased he was, and since space was expensive, museums and art galleries tended to be very crowded places.

The Historisches Museum in Frankfurt-am-Main has a watercolour of the picture gallery belonging to the Frankfurt merchant, Johann Valentin Prehn. It was painted in 1829 and shows how one naturally tidy-minded man had attempted to keep the space problem under control and yet at the same time have all his collection on view in a single large room. His solution was to buy only small and medium-sized pictures.

Ferdinand Franz Wallraf, Baron Hüpsch, was less successful. The extreme disorder of his collections in Cologne was commented on by Wilhelm Grimm in 1815, in a letter to Achim von Arnim. 'Wallraf's collections are remarkable,' he wrote, 'but the muddle is so dreadful that it is only possible to pick out an odd item here and there. The lack of peace and calm, as Hüpsch shuffles objects about, is most disturbing.'[11]

This contrasted strongly with what Goethe found when he visited the collections of Adam Friedrich Oeser at Leipzig. Everything here was 'tastefully, simply and methodically arranged, so that a great deal was got into one small room. The furniture, cupboards and portfolios were elegant, restrained and uncrowded.'[12]

It is a debatable point as to which of two kinds of museum the visitor finds most exhausting and frustrating – the small, crowded museum, in which he has to do very little walking but a great deal of peering and mental sorting; and the large, orderly museum in which everything is clear and regimented, but where room passes into room in an apparently never-ending sequence and where one's brain, spirit and feet try to meet an impossible challenge. The difficulty which faces the historian is that, until very recently, it has not been fashionable or respectable to set down one's feelings of weariness on paper for posterity to read. The remarkable thing about professional museum visitors is their stamina. They never seem to tire. From about the 1820s onwards they begin to criticise the way the collection is arranged, or labelled, or lit, the inconvenience of the opening hours, the behaviour of the attendants. What is very rare is any confession of physical weakness.

At all times, the connoisseurs and the professional critics

have visited exhibitions and galleries in a different spirit and
with a different notion of enjoyment from the general public.
How far, it is interesting to wonder, did they see what the man-
in-the-street saw? Suppose, for instance, that we consider the
comments of the German art historian, G. F. Waagen, on the
Elgin marbles, which he saw, as many thousands of other
people did, in the British Museum in 1837.

> I never, perhaps, found so great a difference between a plas-
> ter cast and marble as in these Elgin marbles. The Pentellic
> marble of which they are formed, has a warm yellowish tone,
> and a very fine, and at the same time, a clear grain, by which
> these sculptures have extraordinary animation, and peculiar
> solidarity. The block for instance, of which the famous
> horse's head is made, has absolutely a bony appearance, and
> its sharp flat treatment has a charm, of which the plaster cast
> gives no notion. It produces the impression as if it were the
> petrified original horse that issued from the hand of the god,
> from which all real horses have more or less degenerated, and
> is a most splendid justification of the reputation which
> Phidias enjoyed among the ancients as a sculptor of horses.
> This head, as well as all the statues from the two pediments of
> the Parthenon – of which, partly from the importance of the
> place they occupy, partly from the beauty of the work, it may
> be assumed with the greatest probability that they are from
> the hand of Phidias himself – stand in a long line in the
> middle of the hall in the order, which it is partly conjectured
> they were originally arranged. As the window is immediately
> over them, they unfortunately do not afford any contrasts of
> decided masses of light and shade.[13]

Waagen arrived at the British Museum with exceptional ad-
vantages. He had already seen and studied casts of these sculptures, he knew about Phidias and about the qualities of
Pentellic marble and, most important, he had the education,
the experience and the sensitivity which allowed him to understand the nature of the artist's achievement, and to see how this
was belittled by the way in which the sculptures were arranged
and lit in the museum. The more ordinary visitor would have
been impressed by the size and possibly the vigour of what he
saw and the story of how the marbles were filched from the Par-

thenon by British cunning and determination might well have appealed to him. He would almost certainly not have been in a position to compare these horses with those depicted by other sculptors, or to assess the formidable skill of the composition. The Elgin Marbles were just one item in his tour of the Museum, and by the time he had finished with the Greek and Roman antiquities he had probably had enough of marble for the moment.

He would, one might guess, have understood Waagen's remarks about the National Gallery rather better. The Gallery at this time was in a temporary home in Pall Mall, and the pictures could be seen, free of charge, from 10 to 4 on Mondays, Tuesdays, Wednesdays and Thursdays. Whether anyone, expert or not, could have derived much pleasure from a visit is doubtful, since, as Waagen pointed out, 'the four rooms have a dirty appearance; and with great depth and so little light that most of the pictures are but imperfectly seen. They are hung without any arrangement as chance has decided.'[14]

During the 1820s and 1830s, newspapers in all the major European countries began to devote much more attention to art criticism and by the 1850s *The Times*, for example, was publishing what were, in effect, art leaders. In 1850 it directed its gaze on the newly opened Vernon Gallery at Marlborough House. The gallery here was confined to works by British artists and it was accessible, free of charge, to 'the entire public of every rank and class throughout this metropolis'. Conditions were, however, far from good.

> The rooms are most of them unfortunately small for any public purpose [wrote *The Times'* critic], and will be found when crowded to be ill ventilated. The light is in almost all instances, bad, but especially in the eastern and western rooms of the suite, the windows being narrow and placed low down in the walls, so that all the larger paintings are lit from below. In the front rooms the light is somewhat stronger, but of course it serves only for the side walls. In short, while this change serves to show how much the effect of this collection may be increased even by a partial amelioration, it reminds us more forcibly than ever that the time is come when an ample and appropriate edifice is more than ever required to

meet the just expectations of both our artists and of the public.[15]

The pictures 'present a pleasing and creditable proof of what has been done among ourselves', but 'a more strict selection' would have been welcome. Things would no doubt improve with time, and meanwhile *The Times* looked down from its pedestal to 'congratulate the public on their speedy access to a new pleasure which is in every sense their own'.

The Times was not given to mincing its words. An exhibition of works by members of the Society of British Artists, at the Suffolk Street Gallery 'contains, as usual, a very large proportion of works upon which it is needless – and it might be unpleasant to dwell'[16] and at the gallery in Bridgewater House, opened to the public in June 1851, the architect, Barry, 'has not been successful in the distribution of light, or in the amount of space provided for the pictures'.[17] Due to windows being put in the wrong place and at the wrong angle, there was 'a certain amount of reflection on the walls below, which affects the eye disagreeably when the spectator stands in the middle of the room'. The impression is given that Barry would have done well to consult *The Times* before setting to work.

What changed the attitude of museum curators to the public in a fundamental way was not *The Times* or the opinions and skill of prominent architects, but the beginning of the long succession of world's fairs,[18] marked by the Great Exhibition in London in 1851. From then until the outbreak of the 1914–18 war, these international exhibitions, on both sides of the Atlantic, gave museums a social power that they had never had before. They attracted very large numbers of visitors and they compelled both governments and the leaders of fashion and taste to recognise that the sciences and the useful arts were the proper concern of the community as a whole. Formal learning and social needs were brought closer together and the definition of culture was considerably, if belatedly and inadequately, broadened. The international exhibitions were, of course, commercial enterprises and they were required to make as much money as possible, but their importance extended far beyond mere business success. As T. R. Adam has said, 'they opened the way for the renaissance of the modern museum in terms of dramatic displays relevant to the social life of the community'.[19]

The proposal to make the Great Exhibition free to all comers produced misgivings and fears. The size of the building and the range and value of the exhibits were beyond all previous experience. This was display and planning on a scale never before attempted and nobody knew how the public was likely to react. A letter to *The Times* signed 'A Mechanic', expressed feelings that were not peculiar to the writer.

> Sir [it began], in common with all well-disposed persons, I am truly concerned by the suggestion of Mr. Paxton for opening the Exhibition of Industry free to all comers. Surely Mr. Paxton can have very little knowledge of a 'London mob', for to such, most assuredly, would the Exhibition be delivered over.
>
> Nor could there be a greater blow and discouragement to the preparations now being made to visit the Crystal Palace by thousands, to whom the admission fee, compared with their other expenses, is of the most trifling moment, insuring, as it would, a comparatively free and uninterrupted inspection.
>
> What the exhibitors will think of Mr. Paxton's proposal I don't pretend to say, but, for myself, were I an exhibitor of any valuable articles, such as jewellery, gold and silver workmanship, shawls, etc., I should be inclined to withdraw my application for space, preferring my name as an artisan or manufacturer remaining in obscurity to trusting my handwork to the tender mercies and chances of a 'free' public.
>
> Sir, I am one of the humbler class, and, unfortunately, am somewhat acquainted with the character of a 'London mob', a *materiel* once cited (and there will be no want of inciters) and goodbye to all rules of *meum* and *tuum*.
>
> Again, how many of the gentler sex, and the exemplary wives and daughters of our honest artisans, are looking forward to this treat but would, or even could attempt it, if 'free' to 'his majesty the mob'?[20]

'A Mechanic''s answer to the frightening possibilities was to restrict free entrance to the end of the period when the Exhibition was open. If the mob then destroyed or stole the exhibits, or created danger and chaos, the problem would be much less serious, because by that time the well-behaved sections of the community would have had a chance to enjoy themselves in peace.

However, entrance remained free throughout, riots and brawls failed to occur and damage and theft proved to be very minor worries. The working people of Britain turned out to be better disciplined and more intelligent than was generally considered possible, or proper. But they had their difficulties, as one of *The Times*' more unconventional correspondents pointed out.

> Sir, after Master reads *The Times* I get it, and we are pleased with what you says about the Exhibition, and we servants and other middleing folks. And we shold be glad if you would print that but for a very few servants cant come up to the Exhibition, for the trains dont help us a bit. One excursion train goes up in a morning and comes back at night, and another takes five days; so neither ant any use – one is too short, and the other too long; Master cant spare us, and we cant spare the monney. We wont three days insted of five, and we hope you will tell the Great Western so.
>
> I remain, yours humbly,
>
> A COUNTRY GROOM
>
> Only one servant out of use five has been up yet, and we cant if it isent altered. If you alter this and put it in propper it will do good.[21]

The large international exhibitions were children of the railway age. Without railways to transport materials, machinery and visitors, the organisation would have been impossible. But although, as the letter just quoted makes clear, even quite humble people were prepared to make long journeys to visit these exhibitions and to see the new technical wonders on display there, there were very practical limitations on what was possible. Middle-class people may have been able to come a couple of hundred miles and stay one or two nights, but most members of the working classes had to be home the same night. For this reason, exhibitions in the provinces were more important than people in Paris, London, Vienna and other capital cities were inclined to admit or understand. New American agricultural machinery, for instance, may have made a great impression at the Great Exhibition in London, but it was in Norfolk and Devon that it had to be publicised, sold, explained and used.

It is for this reason that agricultural shows were of immense significance. They provided an opportunity for farm and household equipment to be carefully studied and, in many cases, seen in action; and, in at least one instance, they allowed rural people to see, for the first time in their lives, good paintings and collections of applied art. The pioneer here was the Bath and West of England Society, which began an Arts and Manufactures Department at its Barnstaple Show in 1853. A special building was designed, 100 feet long and 40 feet wide, potential exhibitors were circularised – manufacturers had to pay to show their goods – and the result was a collection of exhibits of cutlery, harness, furniture, decorative ironwork, guns, glass, pottery and lamps. One of the major firms represented was Price's Patent Candle Company, with a display of candle-manufacture and the ingredients used in it. The recently established Department of Science and Art in South Kensington, later to become the Victoria and Albert Museum, lent a specially assembled collection of pottery.

> This Museum [reported the organising committee] is rich in specimens of ancient pottery, and with the assistance of the catalogue, and under the guidance of Mr. Worsnop, the intelligent and obliging curator, it will afford visitors an opportunity of making acquaintance with the 'Majolica', 'Fayence', 'Palissy', and most of the other wares which have at various times been produced in Europe, as well as to see genuine specimens of Oriental manufacture.[22]

At Barnstaple, the Society put on exhibition a number of drawings by Turner, 'some of whose relations were actually living in Barnstaple as artisans, and came to look and wonder'. In succeeding years, the more distinguished artists represented included Holman Hunt, Frith, David Cox, Angelica Kauffman and Sir Joshua Reynolds. Most of the pictures were lent by people living in the area where the Show was taking place, four of the Reynolds shown at Plymouth in 1872, for instance, coming from the Earl of Morley's house at Saltram, and two more from the Earl of Mount Edgcumbe. 'It is needless to say', reported the Society in connexion with the Plymouth Show, 'that this magnificent Loan Collection was visited by eager crowds each day of the exhibition, most of whom witnessed perhaps for the first time in their lives those grand works of English art of which this country is so justly proud.'[23]

The Society's Arts and Manufactures Department, under its far-sighted chairman, Sir Thomas Dyke Acland, worked to a firmly-held policy. In selecting the examples of 'industrial art', the principles were:

> Firstly, that ornament should be consistent with the construction required for real use, not the construction made to fit to a pattern chosen for the sake of ornament, just as a horse's shoe should be made to fit the foot, not the foot be fitted to a ready-made shoe. The second principle is that the natural qualities of the material should be considered in framing the design, whether for construction or ornament, the opposite error being very common, namely, to borrow patterns invented by the workers in stone, wood or iron, and attempt to reproduce the pattern in some material for which it was not intended. Each material has its own natural qualities, and therefore its own style.[24]

The application of this philosophy was, by any reasonable definition, educational work. To bring handicrafts, factory products and fine art of high quality to the attention of tens of thousands of people of very mixed educational attainment each year was a remarkable achievement, and one not paralleled during the mid-Victorian period either by the formal educational system or by museums. Visitors to agricultural shows came to enjoy themselves and to pick up new ideas in an atmosphere that was familiar, noisy and friendly. They were not at all in the position of uneducated people in museums and, even more, art galleries.

For this reason, Mr Worsnop, 'of the South Kensington Museum', to whom reference has already been made, had no hesitation in declaring in 1869 that the Bath and West of England Society and Southern Counties Association is one of the great Art teachers of the day. It brings annually before a class of society, that cannot be reached in any other way, a varied and valuable collection of oil-paintings, water-colour drawings, and works of ornamental art, seldom surpassed by exhibitions of a more stationary and lasting character; thereby awakening thoughts that otherwise might not have existed.[25]

At that year's Southampton Show, Mr Worsnop had overheard a remark which illustrated this. 'An agriculturist of the humblest class, on first entering the "Arts Department", exclaimed, "Well, I did not think that there were so many pictures in the world!" Perhaps he had not thought about the subject at all; but the Society's exhibition had made him think, and enlightened his mind on one point at least, quantity.'[26] This simple peasant was not, in Mr Worsnop's opinion, the kind of man who was likely to patronise museums. 'Local museums', he said, 'are, generally speaking, places so cold and repelling in their nature, that, if a person have the hardihood to enter them, he cannot fail to be struck by the chilling nature of their contents, the unsatisfactory method of lighting, and the death-like stillness that reigns.'[27]

It is only comparatively recently that it has become respectable to consider pleasure and education as closely linked, both for children and for adults. The Arts Department of the Bath and West Society was many years ahead of its time. The educational mission of most of the museum founders and directors of the second half of the nineteenth century had a sternly disciplined and not infrequently religious flavour about it. Their museums were temples of self-improvement, which made few concessions to human frailty and which were, as Worsnop rightly said, all too often cold, chilling and repelling.

It is interesting to wonder how far Worsnop would have felt these adjectives could be applied to his own museum, which had been opened in its first home, Marlborough House, in 1852. The collections there were arranged mainly according to the material from which the objects were made – metal, textiles, wood and so on. Watercolours of the various rooms, painted by W. L. Casey in 1856 and 1857, give a good idea of how the exhibits were arranged, but they contain no people, so that we are unable to guess at what visitors found most interesting. The existing room-divisions at Marlborough House had, of course, to be respected and the museum, as a result, appears distinctly cramped, with giant free-standing cases reaching two-thirds of the way to the ceiling and many pieces placed too far away to allow close or detailed inspection. The floorboards are left bare and there is no evidence of any heating or artificial lighting.

Everything is, however, very orderly, although no form of labelling is apparent, and the visitor who was already well briefed and who knew what to look for would probably have found a great deal to interest him. The general public would certainly have received an overall impression of grandeur and riches, but how meaningful the collections would have been beyond that it is very difficult to say. At Marlborough House no seats were provided and no refreshment room. Self-education here demanded strength and stamina. In the new buildings at South Kensington, however, completed in 1857, there were large refreshment rooms from the beginning, an indication that the visitors were to be regarded as human and that the Museum saw itself to some extent as a place of entertainment and relaxation.

3
MUSEUMS AS EDUCATIONAL INSTRUMENTS

'The primary purpose and function of a museum and its exhibits is to educate', wrote Lothar P. Witteborg, of the American Museum of Natural History in 1958.

To achieve this end at a natural history museum, exhibits should be planned for which actual life is illustrated and in which native skills and cultures are displayed. Nothing should be shown merely because it is ancient or has curiosity value. Specimens, reconstructions and processes should be exhibited because they have the authentic power to open the visitors' eyes to the movement and meaning of the stream of life. The natural history museum should take elements from nature and from life itself along with theories, concepts, and philosophies achieved through scientific research, and combine them all into a meaningful presentation which tells a story. Within this basic philosophy it is the job of the museum designer and exhibit specialist to arrange the material into an aesthetically pleasing exhibit.[1]

Most museum professionals over the age of forty would probably agree with this, in general terms, but the passage makes certain assumptions, which are nowadays being increasingly challenged. Is 'telling a story' the best way of achieving 'meaningful presentation'? Are people who have become accustomed to the impressionistic methods of television and the cinema willing to accept the established tradition of moving from one piece of information to another in a logical sequence? Why should a museum put such an enormous emphasis on acquiring information? Is 'education' totally unconnected with attitudes and emotions? Who is to say what thoughts are going through the head of a museum visitor as he gazes at a stuffed gorilla? Or what thoughts should be going through his head? Are the only reputable thoughts those which are based on 'scientific research'? Is it right for museums to attempt to control people's responses?

The present writer recalls an incident fifteen years ago in Bristol which illustrates admirably that, however determined and confident designers and planners may be, members of the public will react in their own individual, wilful, human way to what is set in front of them. The occasion in question was an exhibition to illustrate the workings and principles of nuclear reactors, arranged by the Central Electricity Generating Board. There were models, diagrams, photographs, captions, everything to please the heart of the most scientifically-minded educator. A number of visitors were asked on leaving what they had learnt from the exhibition, what had interested them. One young man said he had been there three times already, but not for any scientific reasons. The exhibition had taught him absolutely nothing about physics or engineering, subjects to which he was totally dead. He was an artist, he said, and he was attracted by the beautiful shapes of the reactors and other parts of the installations. The Central Electricity Generating Board was neither pleased nor flattered. They were in the electricity business, not the shapes business, and their exhibition designers had failed them.

There is, of course, nothing wrong with ideals or with the wish to provide people with opportunities to educate themselves. What is not immoral, but absurd, is the belief that one can select, arrange and present objects in such a way that everyone who sees them will and should respond in a prescribed and guaranteed manner. It is not always easy to decide what the men who established and ran museums were trying to do. Was their aim to condition visitors, to mould and direct their thoughts and attitudes? Or were they content to let the collections speak for themselves, reckoning that the general effect would be beneficial and that people would leave the museum better than when they went in?

Sir John Soane appears to have planned his museum in London in the hope that what pleased and inspired him might please other people too. The Museum,[2] at his house in Lincoln's Inn Fields, was inaugurated immediately after his death in 1837, but for some years before that its philosophy and organisation had been forming themselves in his mind. His object was certainly educational, 'the Promotion of the Study of Architecture and the Allied Arts', and to provide the framework for this his private Act of Parliament, passed in 1833, laid down that free admission to the house

> should be given at least two days in every week throughout the months of April, May and June, and at such other times in the same or any other months as the said Trustees shall direct, to Amateurs and Students in Painting, Sculpture, and Architecture, and to such other persons as shall apply for and obtain admission thereto.

At the same time, he prepared, with the co-operation of Mrs Barbara Hofland, a brief guidebook[3] to lead visitors through the house and its collections. In the Exordium to the guide, Sir John explained what he was hoping to achieve.

> However carefully arranged as to general effect, or advantageously displayed as to light and shadow, the works of Art here described may be, it is obvious, that in so extensive and various a Collection, some objects of great interest may require that the eye should be expressly directed to them. Without such guidance, many of the smaller Models and Sculptures might be overlooked, by those who will delight in tracing their happy conception and delicate workmanship, when thus led to them as subjects for consideration. But besides my hope of being a useful guide to those who visit the House and Museum, and of conveying to those who have not seen them some idea of the manner in which the works of Art are arranged and the different effects are produced, I was influenced by other motives in printing the following Description.
> One of the objects I had in view was to shew, partly by graphic illustrations, the union and close connection between Painting, Sculpture, and Architecture – Music and Poetry; – another purpose is, the natural desire of leaving these works of Art subject as little as possible to the chance of their being

removed from the positions relatively assigned to them; they having been arranged as studies for my own mind, and being intended similarly to benefit the Artists of future generations.

This Description however was chiefly written for the advantage of the Architect, who will, I trust, become sensible, that every work of Art which awakens his ideas, stimulates his industry, purifies his tastes or gives solidity to his judgment, is to him a valuable instructor; and may probably lay the foundation of that knowledge, which may enable him to become an ornament and benefit to his Country.

The relative positions of the various items on display were to be fixed and unalterable for all time. They had been established, as Sir John expressed it, 'as studies for my own mind' and he hoped 'the Artists of future generations' would find the arrangement helpful. It is important to notice that he was making no attempt to tell visitors what they should see or think. They were free agents, capable of forming their own opinions on what was set before them. A good painting or a good piece of music must communicate, if it communicated at all, personally. Sir John knew, and believed each visitor to the Museum would know, too, that 'every work of Art which awakens his ideas, stimulates his industry, purifies his taste or gives solidity to his judgment, is to him a valuable instructor'. The key words are 'to him'. The Museum succeeded, and justified itself, by helping individuals to educate themselves. It was not in the mass-instruction business.

One can, of course, wish to condition people's emotions without in the least intending to determine which facts they shall absorb, and in what order or pattern. In 1815 Ludwig I of Bavaria engaged the architect, Wittelsbach, to design him a new sculpture gallery in Munich.[4] They were anxious to avoid being didactic. For this reason there was to be no 'cynical simplicity', but rather a calculated splendour 'which could communicate to the observer the concept of reverence which should be paid to the masterpieces of antiquity'. In the Glyptothek, atmosphere was more important than facts. There were no descriptive labels or catalogues, no seats and no rails to keep visitors away from the exhibits. The attendants were dressed in magnificent liveries, to make it clear that this was no ordinary place, and on occasional evenings the King entertained special guests to refreshments and led them on a torchlight tour round the galleries.

The attitude of Frederick William III of Prussia was not disimilar. In 1815, when he was commissioning what was later known as the Old Museum in Berlin, he announced that his aim was to bring about the 'honouring of the arts'. The statues and paintings were to be presented in such a way as to create among those who saw them 'a mood of sacred solemnity'. In the Rotunda, the Greek and Roman statues were placed on very tall pedestals, so that visitors had to look up to them.[5]

At the early nineteenth-century Folkwang Museum at Hagen, the curator, Osthaus, saw the main purpose of a collection of works of art to be the awakening of reverence and devotion. Museums were temples and their directors priests, to be addressed as such. In a age when the appeal of religion had faded, art had to take its place.

'Religion' can, of course, be interpreted in many different ways. In 1837, when Dr F. B. von Siebold opened his ethnographical collection in Leiden to the public, he published a paper called 'On the suitability and usefulness of an Ethnographical Museum in the Netherlands'. In it he wrote:

> Man in his manifold development under foreign climates is the principal subject of an ethnographical museum. An entertaining and instructive and therefore useful occupation is provided by following the inhabitants of foreign countries and studying their peculiarities. It is even a moral, religious work to occupy oneself in this way with one's fellow-man, to learn the good qualities in him and to get nearer to his self by becoming more familiar with that alien exterior which frequently repels us without our knowing why.[6]

In 1837 such an aim was many years ahead of its time, but it has continued to be the foundation of the Museum's policy and in the 1960s it was restated in these terms:

> When a museum like the National Museum of Ethnology tries to draw the attention of a larger public to the life and works of fellow-men in far-off parts of the world, it does so in the first instance not to imbue this public with factual

knowledge, but to make it conscious of the limitations created by its own feelings of prejudice towards this strange world of behaviour. The visitor may then understand the reasons for his own reactions, and learn how to meet the other man with a more open mind. The visitor will, of course, adhere to his own pattern of life and culture, but he may nevertheless learn to understand the undesirability of playing hide-and-seek behind his own fixed patterns to protect himself against imagined foreign hostility.[7]

This necessarily involves saying, and believing, that one's own culture is only one of many, that no country is better or worse than another, that museums which try to foster an aggressive national consciousness are intolerant and dangerous. Such a creed was altogether opposed to the philosophy behind nineteenth-century nationalism and imperialism.

In both France and Germany, museums were often founded in order to encourage patriotic feelings. In Bonn, the Museum of Antiquities of the Fatherland (Museum Vaterländischer Altentümer) was established, 'so that, through education and affection, the citizens should develop an enthusiastic interest in the German past and a willingness to work towards the growth and strengthening of the State'.[8]

It is easy to smile at the seriousness with which the Germans took their museums last century. At an exhibition held in the newly opened Zeughaus in Berlin in 1844 it was decided to guide the public along a predetermined route through the galleries, so that they should see everything in the correct order and miss nothing. The design of the building made it difficult to achieve this by notices and sequence of doors and corridors, so the visitors were moved along in the right direction by means of spoken or shouted commands, in proper Prussian military fashion.

One can wander round these vast Victorian palace-museums in Germany, Austria, Hungary, Italy, France and elsewhere, and marvel that there was never any shortage of material to put in them. Archaeological and ethnographical items were always to be had in abundance. Excavations were going on in steadily increasing numbers throughout Europe and the Middle East. Travellers and explorers were bringing back enormous quantities of what can only be called loot from Africa, South America, China, Japan and the Pacific islands. Botanists, zoologists and geologists were foraging all over the world and shipping their finds back to their motherlands. The problem, which became more acute each year, was what to do with it all. How was it to be sifted, housed and arranged and made meaningful?

The worst results were to be seen in natural history collections, mainly because the art of taxidermy was not well understood and, as a result, a high proportion of the birds and animals on display were shown in unnatural and unattractive attitudes or, even worse, simply rotted away. In 1898 Sir William Flower, Director of the Natural History Museum in London, and a much-travelled man, took stock of what was happening and delivered an unflattering verdict. Overcrowding, he declared, was general, and to be deplored. 'If an object is worth putting into a gallery at all,' he said, 'it is worth such a position as will enable it to be seen'.[9] He makes pungent comments on 'the sadly-neglected art of taxidermy' and notes that it

> continues to fill the cases of most of our museums with wretched and repulsive caricatures of mammals and birds, out of all natural proportion, shrunken here and bloated there, and in attitudes absolutely impossible for the creature to have assumed when alive.

This was certainly true, although whether visitors to these museums were as worried as Sir William himself is open to doubt. In any case, at least one curator later found a way of using his worst horrors to good purpose. In the 1930s Dr Barbour assumed control of the natural history collections at the Peabody Museum, collections which had been built up over more than a century. His first inclination was to consign practically everything to the bonfire, but before he moved into action, a more creative idea occurred to him.

> I found that some of the worst of the junk had a sentimental value which could not be left out of consideration, so I saved some of the relics and cudgelled my brain for some use to which they might be put. One of the specimens to which I refer was a mounted King Penguin. Now if you search

throughout the museums of the world there is no possibility whatsoever that you would have been able to find another penguin so utterly hideous, so vilely mounted, as my Salem candidate for salvage. I thought to myself, 'What does this bally thing show?' It suddenly occurred to me, 'Unquestionably it shows what was considered a good specimen, well worthy of exhibition, a treasured relic indeed, in the eyes of those who visited the Peabody Museum, say, 125 years ago'.

This gave me an idea. I put it on exhibition and set beside it a magnificent Emperor Penguin which I wheedled out of my friend Dr Alexander Wetmore, Director of the United States National Museum in Washington. This penguin, taken on Byrd's last expedition to the South Pole, is the last word in lifelike artistry, an example of the incredible perfection which the art of taxidermy has reached today. The old penguin, labelled to set forth its history (it was the first bird of its kind ever to reach an American museum), with the other placed alongside, made an exhibit of taxidermy then and now which is certainly vivid, and one which has been eagerly sought out and examined by visitors ever since the new hall in the Salem Museum was opened.[10]

Sir William Flower might well have done the same; but as it is, his passion for realism and good workmanship has deprived us of the opportunity to see some of the items which must have delighted Londoners during the Victorian period.

One of the difficulties which beset museums, local authorities and, in some instances, the State, especially during the second half of the nineteenth century, was that wealthy men were increasingly bequeathing their collections, usually to the town where they lived, with instructions that these collections were to be used for educational or scientific purposes. The problem then was to find a suitable building and to raise sufficient money to pay the necessary staff and meet the running expenses. Private collectors had a way of assuming that what was decreed in one's will was automatically possible, that the gift itself was everything.

In Dresden, for instance, Dr Gustav Klemm had built up a large, systematically-arranged ethnographical collection. On his death, in 1869, his heirs and executors offered it for sale, in accordance with his wishes, in order that it should become the nucleus of a major anthropological museum. A committee was set up in Leipzig, to undertake an appeal for funds. An announcement in the *Leipziger Zeitung*[11] explained that the collection was of great scientific value and that the price asked for it was remarkably low. In addition to asking for money, the committee invited members of the public, especially 'Germans living abroad', to make gifts of suitable material, in order that the museum could be enlarged and made more useful. Klemm had, so to speak, primed the pump.

The size and range of his collection would have seemed enormous fifty years earlier, but, in 1869 and with the new German insistence on comprehensive, scientific museums, it was no more than a core, around which an adequate museum might be developed. The catalogue revealed the following details.[12]

Category	Number of items
Anthropology, food, narcotics, fire and fuel	520
Weapons, tools	2,450
Jewellery, ornaments	1,600
Clothing	1,200
Pots, jars and other vessels	2,500
Household equipment	1,050
Vehicles	300
Musical instruments	180
Religious items	2,500
Art	1,600
History of writing	550
Weights and measures, coins	1,400
Public life	10
Relics	80
Total	15,940

In the form in which Gustav Klemm bequeathed it, his excellent collection was of very limited educational value, because it was not in a building where even a limited public could use it. The same could be said of a remarkable collection of art and archaeology formed in Rome by Augustus Kestner,[13] who was Ambassador in Rome for the Kingdom of Hannover and succeeded Bunsen in 1838 as Director of the Archaeological Institute there. In his will, he said he had originally intended to leave his collection to the University of Göttingen, 'so that it could stimulate and nourish the studies of young talents', but that he gradually came to feel that he 'could not bear the thought of it disappearing from the eyes of my dear relations in Hannover'.

After his death, the collection was transferred from Rome and installed in the house of his nephew, Hermann Kestner. He arranged for the City of Hannover to take the collection, in 1884, and to put up a suitable building to accommodate it. Meanwhile, a Hannover printer and senator, Friedrich Culemann, had died and bequeathed his collection of early books, paintings and medieval art to the City; or rather, given them the first chance to buy it. The Kestner and Culemann collections were amalgamated and Hannover found itself with an excellent public museum, which was not so much intended or planned as made inevitable by circumstances.

The great national museum of applied art in Berlin had origins of quite a different kind. Opened in 1881, it was directly inspired by the South Kensington Museum, in London,[14] and many of the original exhibits came on loan from British collections. It was housed in a new building, huge, square and utilitarian.

> The art treasures already arranged within its walls [it was reported], have been derived from various public and private stores, from the State collections that have hitherto partially served the purpose for which the new and more comprehensive museum is now intending, and from the cabinets of Prussian Sovereigns, Princes and other collectors of as liberal hand as mind.[15]

Attached to it was the School of Industrial and Decorative Art, which in 1881 was already being attended by nearly one thousand students. The Museum and the School were regarded as a single closely integrated unit, with the museum providing a rich variety of study material for the students of art and design. A similar concept led to the establishment, in the 1890s, of the Cooper Union Museum in New York. It was the Museum for the Arts of Decoration, a museum to serve the needs of the designer, the artisan and the student. The two sisters, Sarah Cooper Hewitt and Eleanor Garnier Hewitt, who were responsible for setting it up, had seen and admired the collections at the South Kensington Museum and at the Musée des Arts Décoratifs in Paris. They believed that a museum of the same type would help to raise the standard of industrial design in the United States. It was an essentially practical museum, planned, as Calvin S. Hathaway had described it, 'for direct and immediate use by all comers'.[16]

The Cooper Union Museum was remarkable in having an organisation geared to the needs and habits of students, not of a bureaucracy or administration. There were few restrictions and regulations, the atmosphere was informal and it remained open in the evenings. Casual visitors have always been a minority. The collections were intended to serve men and women who earned their living by designing furniture, textiles and other items in daily use.

The Victorians, whether in America or in Europe, placed much emphasis on their museums being 'useful', but there was considerable disagreement as to how this important quality of usefulness was to be measured. For some it meant 'helping people to do their work more effectively'. For others it was 'improving people's general knowledge, providing a more worthy sense of values'. For others again it was 'giving a sense of national purpose, binding the different social classes together'.

The German museums were imbued with a powerful sense of mission. They should, in every possible way, convey to their visitors the message that Germany was strong, great and growing. To those not fortunate enough to be born in Germany, the effect could be nauseating. During the 1870s and 1890s, Thomas Greenwood, for instance, was able to see a number of museums on both sides of the Atlantic. Prussianism was not at all to his taste:

> The most raw student, transplanted from anywhere and placed in a German Art Gallery or the Royal Palaces of Berlin, and the palaces of the petty Princes in the various provinces, if asked his impressions, would probably say that the glorification of powder and shot was the chief characteristic which the pictures of Germany represented.
>
> It is almost impossible to come away from some of the North German Galleries save with sickened feelings. The

truth 'Man's inhumanity to man makes countless thousands mourn' as pictured in much of the so-called North German Art, impresses itself on the mind. There is in it a surfeit of cannon balls, epaulettes, guns, and bloodshed portrayed in terribly realistic colours. Is it not a misnomer to dignify such works with the term Art? It is in the very nature of Art to give repose and rest to the mind and to quicken the finer sensibilities, and it is beyond the possibility of pictures of battles to do this, any more than can a visit to the Arsenal or Military Museum in Berlin convince one that nations are yet within measurable distance of the pruning hook and plough-share period of scripture hope. Whatever plea may be urged for a strong military power in Northern Europe, it is undeniable that both the art and the commerce of the Fatherland have suffered a serious blight from the spirit of military despotism so rampant.[17]

Greenwood's reactions to the Harvard Museum, at Cambridge, Massachusetts, were very different. He was there on a public holiday, in the spring of 1886, and he watched a group of a dozen children looking round the Agassiz Room

> The eldest could not have reached ten and the youngest could not have been more than three years old. There was no hall-keeper to turn them out, and no voice said them nay, and they went from case to case, hand in hand, pointing now and again at some of the objects which specially attracted their attention. They spoke little, but their eyes were full of unspoken words. The eyes of some of them glistened in a way not to be forgotten, for it is well for the world that children have not learned the art of concealing their pleasure. At least two of the children were without shoes and stockings, it may have been from choice more than from necessity, as the day was warm, but the fact remains, and I could not refrain from expressing my admiration for the governing body of any Museum which displayed such catholocity of mind as to permit children so young, unaccompanied by elders, to go in and out of the rooms without let or hindrance.[18]

Greenwood was very interested in watching the behaviour of museum visitors and in trying to guess from the expressions on their faces what they were thinking. One can be sure that if he had found clues of this kind in Berlin he would have reported them. As it was, the formality and stiffness of the atmosphere repelled him. What, he was enquiring, were all these great stone buildings and huge collections for? Was it a case of bigness for the sake of bigness? Or was there something else that the size and the regimentation concealed, something that his dislike of Prussian militarism prevented him from seeing?

The fiftieth anniversary of the foundation of the great Berlin Museum was celebrated on 3 August 1880. An address was presented to the Crown Prince of Germany by the Director General of the Museum and, in reply, his Imperial Highness said to the assembled company and, through the press, to the German nation:

> It is perhaps more important now than ever that we should hold fast to our intellectual possessions, and throw open to our people more and more every day the knowledge of their value and great saving power. This institution is not intended to be anything but a collection of the beautiful things of all times for the use of the well-thinking men of the nation. My wishes are and always will be in favour of directing this institution towards its exalted aims in the sense and spirit to which it owes its foundation.[19]

The idea that a collection of beautiful things should be 'for the use' of visitors is a curious one. What would they use it for? Did 'the well-thinking men of the nation' tour the galleries with a commercial feeling of profit and loss in their minds? Were the statues, pictures and antiquities valued in proportion to the amount of patriotic fervour they aroused? What did the Crown Prince himself mean by 'the value' of the nation's 'intellectual possessions'?

Only a German, perhaps, could guess what other Germans were feeling in a museum, and only a Frenchman could read the faces of Frenchmen. Greenwood certainly believed he could do this for his fellow-countrymen.

> I have [he said] watched minutely the faces of visitors at many an Art Gallery and Museum, especially in the evening, and the faces of the working class visitors have provided a

study in physiognomy so gratifying that I never now enter a
Museum without giving some attention to the faces of the
visitors as well as to the objects in the Museum. How the eyes
light up at some picture, where the 'one touch of nature
makes the whole world kin', and I have more than once seen a
wife with a pale careworn face cling more closely to the arm
of her husband as some picture of child life was being looked
at, or something else suggestive to them, perhaps, of little
fingers lying cold in Mother Earth. Let any opponent of these
institutions open to conviction go some weekday evening or
Sunday to the Birmingham Museum and study for himself
the faces of those who come to see perhaps for the twentieth
time the pictures and other art objects, and he will be convinced. He might notice the weary listlessness of some, but if
he observed faithfully he could hardly fail to notice the deep
interest of others.[20]

Greenwood's philosophy was based on a belief that people
could and should be trusted to educate themselves and that the
business of public bodies was to provide the opportunities for
this process to take place. This concept of the museum's function was, in general, more typical of America than of Europe
during the later nineteenth and early twentieth centuries. Writing in 1968, Eric Larrabee summarised the changes which he
could see taking place at that time:

Until quite recently, American museums thought of themselves primarily as institutions of 'open' education. This view
assumed a general museum-going public desirous of self-
education, for which the simple display of materials would
provide the necessary basis for learning. Increasingly, however, individual museums throughout the country have
become involved in more formal programs of education,
either by direct co-operation with local school systems or
independently. In 1962–63, for example, the American Association of Museums found that as many as 20 per cent of
the 2,752 museums surveyed in a *Statistical Study of Museums in
the U.S. and Canada* were conducting formally organised educational programs for children, while roughly 10 per cent
were engaged in educational programs geared to under-
graduate college students.[21]

One has to remember in this connexion that there are two distinct breeds of people, one of which is driven on mainly by a wish to teach, to instruct, to improve; and the other by a desire to entertain, to please. Each form of motivation can become an obsession or an absurdity. The teacher who believes that education is a serious, even grim business, characterised by hard work and indifference to personal comfort or pleasure, is matched by the public entertainer who sees the emotions as all-important and the mind as very dangerous. Museums, like schools, have swung backwards and forwards between these two extremes. Before 1914, the educators were probably in a majority among museum curators; since then the entertainers have gained a lot of ground.

The Victorians had a great capacity for feeling guilty about enjoying themselves. To justify salvation, they needed to discover a serious purpose behind what might otherwise be considered mere amusement or flippant self-indulgence. An excellent example of this attitude is to be found in a letter written to *The Times* in 1873[22] by a Mr Hodgson Pratt. Writing from the Working Men's Club and Institute Union, in the Strand, he drew attention to the generosity of well-known scholars in guiding groups of working men round some of the London museums on a Saturday afternoon:

> From these visits, numbers of artisans have received some general idea as to the purpose of these several collections, and as to the general scope and value of the branches of knowledge which they represent. In many cases, doubtless, men have thus for the first time been impressed with a sense of the deep interest attached to the pursuit of some department of scientific study, and with a desire to follow up the enquiry, to the great advantage alike of the individual student and of the community to which he belongs.

Mr Pratt thought his Union's Saturday afternoon experiment had so amply proved its worth that the Government should consider turning every public museum in the country into a deliberately planned instrument of adult education for 'those large crowds who annually visit them, and come away as wise as they went'. Assuming a great unsatisfied thirst for knowledge to exist, museums were not fulfilling their potential. 'It has always seemed to me a lamentable waste of opportunity', he wrote, 'that those thousands of men and women should wander, with open eye and mouth, through our grand schools of knowledge, utterly without that which would make these "dry bones" live to their infinite enjoyment and benefit.' Regular popular gallery talks were the answer. At the end of each, 'questions might be answered and the names of books suggested for those who wish to pursue the great topics thus open to their view'.

In an age of enthusiasm for education, when a high proportion of intelligent men and women understood very well the dulling frustration that comes from the awareness that one deserved better than a brief period of elementary schooling, it may have been reasonable to see museums as a liberating force, an opportunity to make up for lost time and wasted years. Nowadays, such an attitude is much less likely to occur, at least in America and Western Europe. Whatever they may have done fifty and a hundred years ago, working-class people today are not educationally thwarted to the extent that their grandparents and great-grandparents were. In general, they are not inclined to snatch eagerly and gratefully at every educational chance that comes their way, regrettable as this may be. Museums today exist in quite a different social, political and psychological context.

In the 1880s it was possible to draw up and publish a list of 'Useful Rules to Keep in Mind on Visiting a Museum', with every confidence that they would meet with a welcome. Today their commonsense and serious purpose would communicate to very few people.

1 Avoid attempting to see too much.
2 Remember that one specimen or one article *well* seen is better than a score of specimens casually inspected.
3 Before entering a Museum ask yourself what it is you wish particularly to see, and confine your attention largely to those specimens. Consult the attendant as to what is specially interesting in each room.
4 Remember that the main object of the specimens is to instruct.
5 Have a note-book with you and record your impressions,

so that on a succeeding visit you may pick up your information where you left off on the previous visit.

6 Introduce in conversation your impressions of what you see in Museums.

7 Consult frequently the technical literature on the special subject in which you are interested.

8 Visit the nearest Museum periodically, and let it be to you an advanced school of self-instruction.

9 Remember there is something new to see every time you go.

10 Make a private collection of *something*. Remember that a collection of postage stamps has many uses.

11 Follow up some special subject of Museum study.

12 See slowly, observe closely, and think much upon what you see.[23]

The description of the local museum as 'an advanced school of self-instruction' summarises the Victorian ideal to perfection. One need not, however, suppose that the ideal was always fulfilled. In Britain, lamented David Murray in 1904, 'museums are regarded too much as mere exhibitions, and are too little employed for practical teaching'.[24] He contrasted this with the situation in Germany where, in his view, 'museums are made the basis of instruction, and every subject which can be made intelligible by means of a museum is provided with a teacher'.

A century ago it was possible for a museum to be a focal point not only of educational ambition and striving, but also of patriotic fervour. In Warsaw, the Museum of Industry and Agriculture, founded in 1875, was one of the Polish Kingdom's institutions designed to protect Polish culture. In the Russian Empire, museums were not subject to government control or police interference, and in the Polish provinces it was consequently possible to give their activities a profoundly patriotic character. The authorities there established museum collections of science and technology, promoted research and organised conferences of all kinds, for the benefit of those engaged in industry, commerce and agriculture. The Museum in Warsaw[25] became a centre of agricultural teaching, with three-year courses of a university standard. It was much used for conferences and seminars, the main object of which was to bring young Polish scientists into closer touch with the national history and traditions and to give them an opportunity to discuss their special subjects in their mother tongue, which they were forbidden to do at the University of Warsaw.

In 1918, with an independent Polish state established, the formal teaching of agricultural subjects was transferred to a specialist college, but throughout the period between the two World Wars the Museum continued to help farmers, by putting on exhibitions to illustrate new techniques, a practice which has been continued since 1964, when the agricultural museum was re-established in new premises at Szreniawa, near Poznań. The new museum, although historical, is defined as 'an institution dealing with scientific and research problems and systematic education, within the social and political framework approved by the state'.

In all the Socialist countries, museums are, in theory, totally integrated with the educational system. In practice, the visitor is likely to discover a number of surprises, especially away from the main cities. But, whether in Poland, Russia or China, the notion that museums might be places in which to while away a wet afternoon not unpleasantly is officially frowned on. In this sense, the Socialists are Victorians. The list of rules for visitors to English museums in the 1880s, which we have quoted above, would translate very easily into Russian or Chinese. It is possible to suspect, however, that, even in Socialist countries, people who visit museums are not always in the purposeful frame of mind which is laid down as appropriate to the occasion. But some part of the offical attitude does undoubtedly rub off, on all but the most eccentric and recalcitrant, more particularly the philosophy that makes clear on all occasions that the past exists in order to illuminate the present, and that every human activity has a social basis. The ideological reorganisation of museums which took place in the Soviet Union during the 1930s provides unmistakeable evidence of a determination to lose no opportunity of reinforcing the Marxist view of history and culture. At the Hermitage, the collection of pictures had been, in the days of Catherine the Great, no more than an accumulation which symbolised immense wealth and power. Subsequently it was rearranged to present the paintings in more or less chronological order and items of obviously inferior merit were relegated to the stores. The Soviet authorities went about the job much more thoroughly, however, and laid down that paintings were to be regarded as no different from any other artefacts. Like machines, costumes or furniture, they were evidence of the way people lived and thought at particular stages of social development. Russian art, for example, illustrated Russian life in its feudal, serf-owning, capitalist and socialist periods.

Other major museums in the Socialist countries have attempted to do the same. One of the most impressive post-war achievements is the Museum for German History, in East Berlin, which was opened in 1952 and deals with the development of German life and culture since 1789, the date of the French Revolution. Its aim was stated to be 'the enlightenment of the people and especially of youth', and[26] the Museum was to be 'a central example of the work to be carried out by historical museums'. With this in mind, German history had been presented as a whole – the politics, the industry, the literature, the wars, the music – decade by decade and with great professional skill. Each room has a text over the entrance, explaining the basic theme of its contents, and visitors are recommended to come more than once and take in a little each time, a procedure which is relatively simple for Berliners but rather more difficult for those who come from a distance.

In the Socialist countries it has been repeated over and over again, on all possible occasions, that culture is an entity in which the whole nation has shares. Culture includes everything that human beings do, make and think. It cannot be fragmented and it is not a veneer on the top of everyday existence. Germans – and similar things are said in Poland, Hungary, Czechoslovakia, Bulgaria – must be given every opportunity to 'discover that their socialist motherland is a rich treasure-house of the human cultural inheritance.'[27]

The Nazis, of course, had said much the same. Their Fatherland Museums and Army Museums were an attempt to awaken and strengthen the national consciousness, and to make people realise the continuity of history in which the individual was no more than a tiny link in an enormous chain. Boys and girls were to be filled with a passionate belief in the destiny in all Germans, whatever their country of residence might be, and with a determination to increase the power and influence of the German Empire. How far this thorough-going attempt succeeded is impossible to say. In any totalitarian regime, it is prudent to pay lip service to what the Government wishes its citizens to believe and we must not expect to find reports of Germans saying the Fatherland Museums were crude, laughable nonsense, or of East Berliners ignoring the political message of the Museum for German History. It is certain, in any case, that members of the older and the younger generation will react very differently, at least in their private thoughts, to the same museum and the same exhibit.

It is interesting to notice how many influential people in the museum field, wherever they may live and work, would like to feel that their museum has a definite purpose. Nowadays they are not content for it to exist, to be well stocked, well arranged. They want it to be for something, and from this point of view the superbly integrated, super-purposeful Socialist museums can be seen as very attractive. 'On the whole,' Alma Wittlin has written, 'the European Museum is an ill-adjusted and in many cases a functionless institution. This fact is revealed both by the attitude to museums of the public which is in fact supposed to benefit from them, and by the views of experts. The public is indifferent to museums.'[28]

Hostility and criticism one can accept and even find stimulating. Indifference, to any impresario, is damning. In America in particular, where salesmanship is highly regarded and highly rewarded, there could be nothing more demoralising for a museum curator than to find that the public had no wish to eat his product. For more than a century, museums have been sold hard in America, quite as hard as they have in the Communist countries, and with encouraging results. 'Here in America,' wrote Margaret Talbot Jackson in 1917, 'a museum is regarded as part of the educational system, and the great contribution that we have made to the development of museum science has been the addition to the duties of the museum official of the important work of teaching Art, not only to those who know that they are interested, but to the school children and others who may be induced to take an interest.'

It would probably be an exaggeration to say that both the

Americans and the Russians dislike the idea that museums may legitimately be places in which to browse, but one could certainly feel that in both these countries the purposeful visitor has a higher prestige and makes the curators feel happier than the person who just strolls around. A more tolerant view is that of that very great curator, Molly Harrison, who was as interested as anyone in helping children to get the most out of their visits to the Geffrye Museum, which she created, but who was not equipped with the frenetic and puritan qualities that have become sadly common among people who run museums nowadays and who are apt to become exceedingly boring with their incessant talk of educational, social or political purpose.

> Museums [she believes] are meeting places, not only for dating on a wet Sunday afternoon, but in more subtle ways. Here values meet; those of the specialist are rubbed against those of the public, children's interests vie with those of adults, the protection of rare objects vies with their display, the individual visitor's concern may be the very opposite of that of the group, whether adult or child.[29]

'An efficient educational Museum', Mr G. Brown Goode told the American Historical Association in 1888, 'may be described as a collection of instructive labels each illustrated by a well-selected specimen'.[30] Such a museum would be a reference library for specialists, and it is exceedingly difficult, if not impossible, to organise a museum to satisfy both the specialist and the lay visitor. Most people do not divide their interests into subject-compartments, however much the educational system may encourage them to do so. As Molly Harrison has said:

> A period room can catch the interest and start a train of thought, where furniture, glass, silver and ceramics arranged in separate cases or separate galleries may mean little or nothing. 'Flora and fauna of the Mediterranean Region' is more understandable, nearer to real experience and a far more enjoyable arrangement than trees, plants, butterflies, birds, snakes or what-you-will arranged separately.[31]

This is a never-ending battle. 'Education' means different things to scholars and to the general public, and before one can decide how well or how badly a museum is carrying out its 'educational function', one must ask 'whose education?' Many critics of museums have completely failed to do this. They assume that there is an absolute concept called 'education', and begin their argument at this point. The results can be ridiculous.

In 1874, for example, *The Times* carried a long and at times violent correspondence which was concerned with the need for a more satisfactory Patent Museum. Readers were assured that 'one of the greatest boons that Her Majesty's Government could bestow on the operative and inventive classes of the country would be to give them a Museum in which they could profitably study the past and present history of inventive genius.'[32] Another correspondent, who had visited and admired the museum of the Conservatoire des Arts et Métiers in Paris, felt that what was required was 'a school in which the student can find the first principles of mechanics illustrated not only in books and diagrams, but in actual working machines'.[33] In Paris this had been already achieved.

> In no place in the world [the correspondent believed] can the student find so much solid information. In no place in the world can the working artisan find information so gathered together that he can understand it. He may not be able to read or write, and the Algebraic formula may be what Greek is to most of us, but he can read the models and profit by their teaching to become a better citizen and a more educated man.

The writers of these letters are dealing in abstractions which may well have had little relation to reality. Who were 'the inventive classes'? What kind of person was 'the student' who was said to derive so much benefit from the collections of the Arts et Métiers? Why was a museum of inventions likely to interest 'the working artisan' more than anybody else? Why should such a collection make him, rather than a clerk or a shopkeeper, 'a better citizen or more educated man'?

Whatever the philosophy of a museum may be, it is obvious that the only people who can be in any way influenced by it are those who are able to visit the collections at the times when they are accessible to visitors. In the nineteenth century, the problem facing those curators who wished to extend the opening hours of their museums in order that working people should be

able to come in the evenings was how to light the galleries suf-
ficiently well to allow the displays to be seen properly. In 1883,
the Secretary of the Working-Men's Lord's Day Rest Association, in London, issued a report[34] on the results of evening
opening at a number of the more important museums.

It was, he noted, twenty-six years since the South Kensington Museum was first opened.

> On three days in each week it has been opened free to the
> public from 10 a.m. to 4, 5 or 6 p.m. at a charge of 6d. The at-
> tendance from June 1857 to March 1883 has been as follows:
> morning visitors – i.e. on six days from 10 a.m. to 4, 5 or 6 p.m.
> (from 42 to 48 hours per week) – 15,304,476; evening visitors –
> i.e. on three days from 6 p.m. to 10 p.m. (12 hours per week) –
> 6,525,746. These figures show that about 30 per cent of all visi-
> tors go during the 12 evening hours per week, when the mu-
> seum is lighted up, as against 70 per cent who go in the 42–48
> hours per week in the day-time. For about 23 years the mu-
> seum was lighted exclusively by gas; for several years past the
> electric light has been gradually supplanting the gas.
>
> The Bethnal-green Museum, situated in a densely popu-
> lated working class district, has been opened since the 25th of
> June, 1872, free to the public three days a week from 10 a.m.
> to 10 p.m. and on three days in each week from 10 a.m. to 4,
> 5 or 6 p.m. The total number of visitors on all days to Sep-
> tember 1883, was 6,879,294; of this 3,338,354 were evening
> visitors. These figures show that nearly half of all the visi-
> tors have been during the 12 evening hours in each week,
> while the other half have visited during the 42 to 48 hours
> per week in the daytime, and that the evening visitors per
> week are nearly four times greater than the day visitors.

The British Museum, as might have been expected, had
shown itself more conservative in these matters. Petitions presented to the Trustees on behalf of 2412 working class organi-
sations had urged that the galleries should be opened between
6 and 10 on at least three weekday evenings each week. For
many years the reply had been that gas-lighting would harm
the exhibits, but in 1883 Sir John Lubbock, M.P., on behalf of
the Trustees, said that evening opening would be possible,
'contingent upon satisfactory arrangements being made for

the electric lighting of the district'. The *Times* report noted that

> the front of the museum, the hall, and the reading room are
> already splendidly lighted with electricity from two engines
> on the premises, and the trustees have ascertained on exact
> estimates that the cost of plant for lighting the whole mu-
> seum, including the reading room, only amounts to £14,194
> and I trust that the day is not far distant when the trustees of
> the British Museum and the National Gallery will open their
> doors till 10 o'clock at night to the millions of visitors who will
> undoubtedly visit them, as they have done to South Kensing-
> ton and Bethnal-green.

The figures quoted above make it clear, beyond all argument,
that, by the end of the nineteenth century, museums were being
visited by large numbers of people who could not be described
as students. Many of them must have come from what Sir
Frederic Kenyon once described as 'unpromising surroundings'.[35] He went on to say that 'the narrower and the
more depressing the immediate aspects of life are, the more is it
necessary, if the mind and the soul are to have a chance to
expand, that the experience which is inaccessible at first hand
should be made obtainable at second hand.' Museums, he
believed, should be planned and arranged so that

> the casual visitor may realise their interest; that he may no
> longer wander wearily through long galleries among objects
> which he does not understand, but may feel at every turn a
> challenge to his curiosity, accompanied by a means of grati-
> fying it. He should go home with an awakened mind and an
> enlarged experience – not merely with a headache.

This would seem to be a very reasonable definition of a public
museum's educational purpose. Unfortunately, there were no
surveys carried out until very recently to discover how many
museum visitors finished up with an awakened mind and an
enlarged experience, and how many with a headache and sore
feet.

Sir William Flower's obituary in the *Yearbook of the Royal
Society*[36] contains a passage which tells us quite a lot about the
devotion and unstuffiness of Victorian public servants at their
best:

While maintaining the high scientific reputation of the National Museum, he continued to popularise the institution and science by taking parties of working men round the museum on Saturdays, and occasionally a distinguished visitor like Dr. Nansen or Professor Virchoff would join the group. Also on Sundays he would take a few busy men, whose occupations prevented their being able to come on week-days, himself unlocking all the doors, so that no 'Sunday labour' was involved. In this way nearly all the Judges were enabled to see the Museum quietly on a Sunday afternoon, the venerable Lord Hannen specially saying what delightful 'refreshment' it gave him after a hard week in the Law Courts! Many ambassadors and foreign ministers, also artists, members of Parliament, and distinguished officers of the Army and Navy, were glad to avail themselves of this privilege, Flower himself explaining the Museum and showing the latest additions; and afterwards they would come on to tea with Lady Flower in Stanhope Gardens.

This was surely museum-going at its most pleasant. It represents, at the same time, what we might term the two-tiered pattern of museum-going. Privileged visitors are able to see the collections in comfort at a time when the ordinary public is excluded – with refreshments with the Director added as social cement. The Director has taken over the patronage-function of the prince who guided favoured people round his art gallery in precisely the same way.

It is interesting to study, in this connexion, H. J. Brooks' painting, *Private View at the Royal Academy, 1888*, now in the National Portrait Gallery, London. The guests shown in the picture include John, Fifth Earl of Spencer; Sir Charles Tennant; Charlotte, Countess Spencer; Miss Margot Tennant (afterwards Mrs Asquith); W. E. Gladstone; Lord Bruton; and Sir W. Agnew. Private views at major exhibitions such as this emphasised two things – the symbolic function of the Academy as a gathering point for the social elite, and, at the same time, the necessity of reserving occasions when members of this elite could visit the gallery without being obliged to see and hear their inferiors. There is no reason to suppose that all, or indeed many, of those present possessed a connoisseur's knowledge of painting. On the contrary, their main anxiety was to show their awareness of current fashion, in painting as in everything else. Their taste and insight are likely to have been unremarkable and their prejudices of the conventional bourgeois kind. Looking at the picture from the more detached viewpoint of nearly a century later, we are free to interpret the not exactly lively expressions on the faces of these distinguished visitors as indicating reverence, bewilderment, boredom, or simply blank indifference. To have pursued the matter at the time would have placed the enquirer utterly and permanently beyond the pale, rather as if one had asked the guests at a wedding or a funeral what thoughts were really going through their heads.

4
ARRANGEMENT AND COMMUNICATION

The public, as a homogeneous unit, does not exist; and it is a waste of time to look for it or to attempt to cater for its needs. For museums, as for libraries, concerts and airlines, there are many publics, each made up of individuals with roughly similar interests, abilities, backgrounds and temperaments. To meet the precise needs of every member of every group is clearly impossible, and if its task is seen in this way, no museum can possibly succeed. What is more reasonable is to try to identify a very few important reasons for visiting a museum and to do one's best to make the arrangement of the museum satisfy these reasons.

The Director of the National Museum of Ethnology at Leiden in the Netherlands distinguishes three motives:[1]

1. *Aesthetic*, the wish to experience beauty;
2. *Romantic or escapist*, 'the urge to leave the everyday world for a short time';
3. *Intellectual*, 'the wish to satisfy a certain thirst for knowledge'.

Each of these, in Dr Pott's view, makes demands on the way material in a museum is presented. The aesthetic approach 'requires a well-thought-out presentation which uses a quiet but neutral background to do justice to a limited number of objects of artistic value, arranged in the most effective way possible'. The romantic approach 'requires that a series of pieces that are interesting for purely human reasons be presented in such a way that they, as it were, invite participation or identification with the society that they represent. In such a setting the human figure should be present, and it should be portrayed as naturalistically as possible.' The intellectual approach 'demands a schematic arrangement which almost literally takes the visitor by the hand and leads him step by step from one suggestion or conclusion to another'.

The ideal visitor, the person in harmony with himself and with his environment, will respond to all three approaches, but he does not appear very often, however much curators may dream of him. One therefore has to content oneself with something rather different, the average visitor, and to try to build up as dependable a picture of him as possible. It is wise, perhaps, to begin with his physique.

'The average American museum visitor, if a man, is about five feet eight and three-quarter inches tall', discovered Arminta Neal, Curator of Graphic Design at the Denver Museum of Natural History;

> and his eye level is five feet four and one-half inches; the average woman is about five feet three and one-quarter inches tall, and her eye level is four feet eleven and three-quarters inches. Thus, the mean adult eye-level height is about five feet two and one-eighth inches. With little eye movement, people usually see and recognize with ease things that are within an approximately elliptical cone of vision, with the apex of the cone at the eye-level height.[1]

This being so,

> the adult museum visitor observes an area only a little over one foot above his own eye level to three feet below it at an average viewing distance of twenty-four to forty-eight inches. Arranging objects and labels above and below these limits places a strain on seldom-used muscles and produces aching backs, tired feet, burning eyes and stiff necks. Some quite large objects, such as totem poles or dinosaurs, will inevitably soar above these viewing limits, and, in this event, the visitor must be permitted space to back far enough away from the object to comprehend it without becoming a case for an orthopedic specialist.

This, one might suggest, is a very American view. It is equally possible that a museum visitor confronted with problems of this order might decide to give up before extreme bodily disturbance set in. But there is certainly no reason why museum curators and designers should not make life as easy for the public as possible. This demands imagination as well as skill. The present writer very well remembers a room in the new Museum of the History of the City of Warsaw in which a number of low, drum-like cases are arranged in rows, with a light suspended above each. The effect is dramatic and the lighting ample, but there is, from the adult visitor's point of view – children are more fortunate – a serious drawback. One bends down, in order to inspect the most interesting items in the cases – they are concerned with education during the German occupation – and eventually, curiosity satisfied, one straightens up. The result is a resounding crack on the head from the light above, which the designers can hardly have intended, but which reduces one's enjoyment of an excellent museum. In time, no doubt, and when sufficient visitors have been hospitalised, common sense will prevail.

In that museum, as with most modern museums, the intention is certainly that people shall look at the individual exhibits. A hundred and fifty years ago this was not necessarily so. Those who founded museums during the first half of the nineteenth century had a fondness for installing the collection in an old palace or in a grand new building designed to look like a palace. This was a matter of snobbery; it echoed the tradition of having a gallery in one's private residence. So the museums went for magnificent staircases, vast high-ceilinged rooms, with frescoed ceilings, and an abundance of marble and carving, all of which had been the panoply of wealth and power in a previous age. It was all extremely expensive, inflexible and intimidating. One does not relax easily in a palace. Those who have inherited such awe-inspiring buildings have had to cope as well as they can. As Molly Harrison has said, 'the solemn hush that used to permeate many museums was as deadening to thought as to feeling, but a livelier, more natural atmosphere is gradually becoming acceptable as huge marble halls are subdivided and ceilings lowered.'[2]

The noisiest museum in the world is probably the Museum of Science and Industry in Chicago, which is filled throughout the day with schoolchildren, all very intent on making the exhibits

work and on extracting the maximum value from what has been
planned as a museum in which the visitors are personally
involved in what is presented to them. The Danish Technical
Museum, at Helsingør, is similarly noisy, and for the same
reason. In both cases, most adults would appreciate a child-free
half-day now and then, but as things are they have, probably
quite rightly, to take second place.

In an art gallery, a reversal of this order of priorities might
well be reasonable Mr Bernard Dunstan, R.A., describing himself as 'an habitué of the National Gallery, in London', claimed[0]
that 'the serious student does surely have a right to peace and
quiet in the museums and galleries which, after all, are more
important to him than they are to anyone else'. He had
observed, with some relief, that 'the National Gallery does not
suffer as much as others do from the blight of the school party',
but elsewhere conditions were so bad that 'it has become very
difficult to concentrate, and in some cases difficult even to see
the exhibits'. The solution, he believed, was to restrict school
parties to one day each week, so that Mr Dunstan and other
'serious students' could find the peace to which he believed they
were entitled. A serious student is frequently, if not usually,
someone who expects to obtain some form of financial gain
from his studies and who is, in this sense, a professional. What
Mr Dunstan is really saying is that museums should recognise
professional artists, writers and scholars to be their most important clients, a claim which many people would dispute.

Personal involvement takes, and should take, a different form
in different kinds of museum. What is right for a museum of
technology is not right for an art gallery. It has been observed,
for instance, that many people enjoy touching and stroking
sculptures. Until comparatively recently, anyone who behaved
in this way would have been reprimanded by an attendant and
quite possibly asked to leave the museum. Modern curators, or
at least some of them, are more indulgent and understanding,
realising that it is unreasonable and frustrating to encourage
visitors to appreciate a highly sensual form of art in a non-
sensual way. But one does not need to make a noise as one
touches a piece of sculpture. An art gallery can be both a par-
ticipating place and a quiet place, and one can, of course, participate with one's eyes as fully and satisfactorily as with one's

fingers and voice.

The nineteenth-century museum assumed that its visitors would participate only with their eyes, although the congestion of the exhibits often made visual appreciation difficult. This was partly because it was customary for all or most of a collection to be on show at the same time. Funds were usually short, especially when so much had been spent on the construction of a grand building, and there was a tendency to devote as much space as possible to exhibition purposes, at the expense of storage and research areas.

This embarrassing congestion continued to be normal until comparatively recently. It was by no means a purely nineteenth century phenomenon. In 1939, recalls Pierre Quarré,[4] the Musée de Dijon was

> a juxtaposition of incongruous collections, with medieval sculptures rubbing shoulders with Renaissance furniture, seventeenth-century engravings, eighteenth-century paintings and nineteenth-century plaster-casts. In the galleries, which were a uniform pink or mauve, pictures were hung one above the other, with no pretence of order, from floor to ceiling. When a new acquisition arrived, nobody took any particular trouble to see if it was a primitive or an eighteenth-century work. The custom was simply to look along the walls to see where there might be room for it and then to push the pictures even closer together to make a space. In this way, a portrait by Manet might find itself with very unsuitable neighbours, such as Marshal Vaillant, whose bust crowned a case containing his innumerable decorations, which presented themselves to the gaze in a quantity rivalled only by those of President Carnot.

What, if anything, the visitor to the museum was supposed to make of all this was probably never considered. The business of an art gallery was to put all its possessions on display, no matter how ridiculous or unprofitable the result might be.

Museums and picture galleries made quite different demands on the available space. In museums, free-standing display cases and exhibits needed large floor areas, while for pictures it was wall space that was important. There was constant argument about the size and position of windows, the best proportions for rooms, heating and artificial lighting.

During the second half of the nineteenth century, new kinds of building materials, equipment and constructional techniques became available to architects commissioned to design museums. Gas lighting was successfully used at the Great Exhibition in 1851 and shortly afterwards at the South Kensington Museum. Electricity was in use at South Kensington in 1882 and at the British Museum in 1890. Exeter Museum (1866) had hot-air central heating and the new Birmingham Museum and Art Gallery (1885) was equipped with lifts and turnstiles.

Paxton's cast-iron and glass construction, which had given his 1851 Crystal Palace such a strong appeal to the public, was handled with considerable caution by other architects, despite its cheapness. The structure of the University Museum at Oxford (1860) was mainly iron and glass, made respectable by Gothic shapes. The Natural History Museum (1880) in London and the Industrial Room (1888) at Birmingham used cast-iron pillars, arches, trusses and girders. In general, however, iron and glass were not treated with Paxton's panache and confidence. They were hidden away behind a conventional exterior.

Whenever there was enough money, museums were richly decorated. At the Fitzwilliam Museum, Cambridge (1848), the overall effect was palatial, with a grand staircase, marble floors and elaborately plastered ceilings. The South Kensington Museum (1860–76) had a superabundance of mosaics, tiles, coloured glass and frescoes. The lecture-theatre façade had carved terracotta figures.

Much of the external decoration was necessitated by the increasing use of roof-lighting, which produced large windowless areas in the external walls. These were relieved by means of niches, statues, friezes, plaques and ornamental panels.

'According to their modern critics', Joyce Jones has written, 'the museums and art galleries of the Victorian period are ill-lit, under-heated, difficult to supervise, costly to maintain and frequently damp, defects which indicate that their architects, preoccupied with historical styles and decoration, were incapable of satisfying the elementary technical requirements of this type of building.'[5]

This criticism is unfair on three counts. Firstly, the architects were experimenting, in order to try to meet the demands of a completely new kind of institution. Secondly, the buildings they produced were for nineteenth, not twentieth-century conditions, and if the twentieth century has failed to provide more suitable replacements, the fault is not that of the original architects. And thirdly, in their own time, these Victorian museums, whether in spite of or because of their buildings, were frequented, regularly and enthusiastically, by very large numbers of ordinary people. To that extent, the architects can quite reasonably be said to have been successful.

However obsolete a building may have become, the obstacles in the way of pulling it down are always very great, especially if it should happen to be of some architectural distinction or if it has become a familiar local landmark.

The Rijksmuseum in Amsterdam is an excellent example of a building that was out of date the day it was opened. As originally planned in 1862, it was to be an architectural embodiment of the history of the Netherlands, and much of this concept survived in the completed building (1885). There were copies of medieval rooms, stained glass windows containing portraits of Dutch worthies, and great names carved in the façade. In the entrance hall were murals depicting scenes from the national past; and throughout the galleries, staircases and corridors were suitable quotations from the Bible and from Holland's most famous poet, Vondel. The total impression was, according to taste, either splendidly patriotic – or ridiculous.

By 1885, when the Museum was finished, the old fusion of art and history was becoming less fashionable, and a greater concentration on the aesthetic aspect of works of art was noticeable. The change was well illustrated by the important Rembrandt exhibition which was held at the Amsterdam Municipal Museum in 1898. The Rijksmuseum co-operated by lending a number of items from its collection, including *The Night Watch*. In the Rijksmuseum, this painting had been hung on the first floor, in a position where it received a somewhat broken north light through a glass roof. In the Municipal Museum it had a side light from the south, which the critics found to be a great deal more satisfactory. After the exhibition and with the return of the painting to the custody of its owners, it was decided to build a special one-storey room, with a cleverly thought-out system of windows and shutters, so that the effect of a wide range of different kinds of light could be carefully studied.[6] These observations revealed that a side light from the south-west gave the best results, and a small gallery was constructed to meet these requirements.

The importance of *The Night Watch* controversy was that it established and publicised the principle that no museum arrangement was fixed and sacred. It could and should be changed as tastes and ideas changed. One should, however, ask 'whose ideas and whose tastes?' An established practice may be shown by experts to be thoroughly bad, but there will be many members of the public, and often many critics as well, who will continue to prefer what has become a trusted and familiar feature of their lives and to fight all change, however obviously beneficial.

An interesting example of this is the public attitude towards the cleaning of pictures. The controversy over this goes back for more than a century. In 1845, the National Gallery in London decided to clean a number of its pictures, including Rubens' *Peace and War*. The removal of accumulated dirt and discoloured varnish showed the paintings in something like their original condition and colours for the first time for many years. Immediately the cleaned pictures were put on public exhibition, Mr Morris Moore wrote to *The Times*, under the penname of 'Verax', charging the Keeper, Sir C. L. Eastlake, with 'wanton destruction' of the pictures. He wrote further to the Trustees, expressing his 'unmixed indignation' at the 'enormities' and 'Vandalisms' that had been committed.

The Trustees therefore asked a number of well-known painters – they included Sir Edwin Landseer – to examine the pictures and to give their opinion on the results of the cleaning. These independent witnesses all pronounced the pictures uninjured. Mr Moore was not placated, however, despite clear evidence that a great many of the other paintings in the Gallery were in urgent need of skilled attention. This statement, he declared to be 'a lie, fabricated by knaves and made current among fools'.

In 1852, Thomas Heaphy wrote to *The Times*[7] in defence of the Trustees. To be convinced that they had acted responsibly and wisely, he said,

it is only necessary for any persons capable of using their fac-
ulties to go and judge for themselves. The change that has
taken place from the removal of years of accumulated and
discoloured varnish, I can only liken to the change from a
yellow November fog to a sunny, May morning. This change
of effect may, possibly, cause some surprise to those who
were familiar with them only under their previous aspect;
but I can state advisedly, and without fear of contradiction,
that there are not two artists of any position or reputation in
the country who will come forward and say that the pictures
have been in the slightest degree injured.

To particularise among the pictures, when all are excellent, would be difficult; but if there are any that have gained
more than others, they are the Paul Veronese, the Claudes,
and the Guercino. The first picture was known to have been
covered with a coating of Spanish liquorice, under the advice
of a picture dealer, because, in the opinion of that gentleman,
it was 'too brilliant'. No matter what the artist who painted it
thought, it was 'too bright' and was accordingly 'liquori-
cised' down to his notion of what an old master ought to be.
This coating of liquorice is now removed, and the public have
the opportunity of judging between the great Venetian painter and the owl-eyed vision of the dealer.

Morris Moore was undoubtedly a foolish and bigoted man,
and a willing tool of the dealers, who found it commercially
helpful to have their old masters looking as old as possible. But
his views were representative of those of many of his fellow Victorians, who felt that several coats of dirt and dulled varnish
made brightly coloured paintings, especially of the Italian and
Spanish schools, seem more English, less foreign, less Catholic.
They felt uneasy when the original picture was revealed, almost
as if it had had its clothes taken off.

Arguments about colour and freshness are closely connected
with arguments about lighting. Nowadays, when the lighting
engineer has become a specialist in his own right and when it is
assumed that the equipment and the skill will be available to
produce any effect the museum designers may wish to see, it is
not easy to understand the passions that were aroused in the
days when lighting was either natural, gas or nothing. It does

not appear to have been widely realised until surprisingly late
in the nineteenth century that, although top-lighting was a sensible and cheap way of helping people to see more museum exhibits, it was extremely unsuitable for most paintings, since the
artist had usually worked with all or most of his light coming
from the side through a window. The habit, frequently followed
by nineteenth-century museum architects, of arranging a
building so that the museum, with side windows, was on the
ground floor and the art gallery, with top-lighting, above, was
not a step forward. The top storey of a museum building is most
suitable for workshops, which are commonly to be found in the
basement.

Yet, even with the extreme flexibility which electric lighting
can give, the battle of the windows continues unabated. The
nineteenth century produces few more violent outpourings
than one, in 1972, from a Past President of the Royal Academy,
Sir Charles Wheeler. Sir Charles was well known for his dislike
of the windowless Hayward Gallery, 'the dreadful Hayward
Gallery'. After visiting an exhibition of Rodin's works there, he
advocated either 'the gallery's demolition, or for windows to be
made in it, if indeed the horrid structure permits it'. As things
were, he felt, 'the exclusion of daylight denigrates its works of
art.' Nothing was right.

> Rodin's bronzes had a dark, polished patina, each piece
> reflecting a hundred ceiling lights which reduced the
> sculptor's breadth of form to littleness, its grandeur to petti-
> ness. The only item one could properly see and appreciate
> was the magnificent 'Balzac' and this because the work had a
> matt surface. . . . Why [he wanted to know] do modern gal-
> lery directors dislike daylight, put in false ceilings and lavish
> money on harsh artificial lighting? The question re-occurred
> to my mind when I first saw the Leonardo Cartoon in a dark-
> ened room at the National Gallery. Its illumination begin-
> ning at the top gradually weakens towards the bottom. It
> appeared so much happier when it could enjoy the daylight
> which it did for nearly two centuries at the Royal Academy.
> Imagine, if you can, the Prado putting Velasquez's 'Las
> Meninas' in a darkened room![8]

In recent years, the multi-storeyed museum has come in for

nearly as much hostile criticism as the multi-storeyed factory or the multi-storeyed shop. These buildings were originally built for social and technical reasons, which no longer apply. In the twentieth century, there is no advantage in pretending that a museum is a palace or a castle. Cars and coaches have made it possible to locate the museum on the outskirts of towns, where land is not so expensive and where a spread-out, single-storeyed museum is practicable. Even those old-established museums in city centres have found, especially in America, that their visitors are no longer drawn from the people who live close at hand. As a result of nearly universal car-ownership, more than half of those who come to a city museum in any given week are strangers.[9] This means that a museum's public has to be divided yet again, this time into casual visitors who want what might be not unjustly described as a quick cultural snack, and local visitors, for whom repeated visits are possible and who have time to interest themselves in a great deal more.

In the traditional type of museum building – and the majority of city museums all over the world are in such buildings – much of the wear and tear on visitors is caused by the need to move from floor to floor. Whether this is by means of a staircase, a lift or an escalator is immaterial. 'Each ascent or descent disrupts the normal flow of a visitor's experiences and activities in the museum and gives him opportunity to become aware of the drain upon his energies.'[10] There is ample evidence to show that, so far as museum visitors are concerned, the higher the fewer; or, in more professional terms, there are 'records of generally diminishing attendance from floor to floor in the upward direction, regardless of the facilities offered for vertical transport, except when very special attractions are offered at upper levels to counteract the trend.'

During the past fifty years, museums all over the world have been forced, often unwillingly, to reconsider their whole policy of acquiring and displaying items, simply because the sheer quantity of material was overwhelming them. This is well illustrated by developments at the Museum of Fine Arts in Boston, which received its charter in 1870. The first museum was opened in 1876, but the collections expanded at such a rate that by the 1890s two extensions had to be added and within a year or two the building was overflowing again. Its policy remains what it was in 1870, 'erecting a Museum for the preservation and exhibition of works of art and making, maintaining and exhibiting collections of such works, and of affording instruction in the Fine Arts.' The difficulty, in Boston as elsewhere, is to find the money with which to carry out such a programme. Despite tax concessions and the generosity of the rich, many museums, in order to raise sufficient funds to stay in business, have departed from their former ideal of private communication between one person and one object and have gone for the mass audience. This has been proved often enough to be a slippery slope, rather than a policy. As one American museum director has pungently put it,

the more a Museum strives for sheer numbers of visitors by providing them with circuses, the more extensive the circus programs must become. The financial returns never reach the cost of the bait. A museum is thus trapped into an endless spiral of activities, a fate very similar to that experienced by a man who has consolidated all his small debts into one big impossible obligation. If attendance figures are the only measure of a museum's worth, why not replace the amiable old gentlemen who serve as guards with girls dressed as Amazons, a classical refinement of topless waitresses?

Art museums are in the hands of directors selected for their ability as showmen. Their public relations men are better paid than their curators. The largest sections of their staff deal with membership, publicity and fund raising.[11]

A new profession and a new language have developed in the attempt to study and increase museum attendances. In the early 1930s one American, Paul Marshall Rea, felt able to state his First General Law of Museum Attendance.

As population increases, attendance at museums in single centers tends to increase at a diminishing rate; and the ratio of attendance to population tends to decrease, at first rapidly and then more slowly. . . .[12] It is measured by the ratio of reported attendance to standard attendance expectation. This efficiency ratio is the fourth and, for the present, the final factor in attendance, and enables us to state that *attendance is the product of a function of population, a function of size, a function of ex-*

penditure, and a function of efficiency. The efficiency ratio of a museum is the measure of the effect of all other attendance factors when the effects of population, size, and expenditure have been evaluated.[13]

There are those – Mr Rea is among them – who believe that, under today's conditions, the best return on investment is to be obtained by decentralisation. The local branch museum is, by his definition, more efficient than the large central museum.

The classic instance of the local neighbourhood museum in a large city is Anacostia, set up in 1967 by the Smithsonian Institution in a black area of Washington. The premises were a disused 400-seat cinema and the man appointed to plan and operate the new museum was a thirty-year-old youth worker, John Kinard. It was a museum such as never existed before, a museum which belonged unmistakeably to the district and which grew naturally from its way of life.

A complete general store, just as existed in Anacostia in the 1890s, occupies one corner. In it is a post office (which we hope to get a license to operate), old metal toys, a butter churn, an ice-cream maker, a coffee grinder and a water pump, all of which can work, and any number of objects of the period from kerosene lamps and flat-irons to posters and advertisements. There is another do-it-yourself area for plastic art, with, at present, volunteer class instruction. There are skeletons of various kinds, some of which can be put together, some disassembled. There is space for temporary art shows. There is a TV monitor system on the stage. Occupying one of the modules is a live zoo with green monkeys, a parrot and a miscellany of animals on loan from the National Zoological Park. A great success was a shoebox museum in an A-frame structure, full of wooden shoeboxes containing bird skins (in celluloid tubes), mammal skins, shells, fossil specimens, pictures and slide projectors for intensive handling and study. A behind-the-scenes museum exhibit of leaf-making, silk-screen techniques, casting and modeling, gives an additional outlet for instruction. All of this, to the tune of crashing hammers, scraping saws and slapping paintbrushes, took form in two and a half months.

The grand opening, attended by an 84-piece band, two

combos, and a block part with speeches and klieg lights, took place on September 15, 1967. A local group of Trail Blazers had painted the nearby fence separating the museum from the next property with a stylish 'primitive' mural of life in Africa. The desolate surrounding lots were spruced up, and one of them decorated temporarily with Uncle Beazley the dinosaur, hero of the story, *The Enormous Egg*.[14]

Anacostia pioneered the concept of a museum without walls, a museum with a creative flow of ideas, exhibits and people be tween the museum and the outside world, a museum which would influence and be influenced by the district in which it was situated. Some people have gone even further than this, seeing the museum of the future as nothing more than a store-house, with exhibits constantly in transit between the central store and a multitude of local sites. In the view of John B. High-tower, Executive Director of the New York State Council on the Arts, this warehousing would not be a serious problem,

> since none of the works will be stored long enough to absorb a disproportionate amount of museum space. More than likely the museum warehouse will be in several late nine-teenth-century buildings since they are the only buildings with the ceiling height to accommodate works for public space except for an occasional railroad terminal or aeroplane hangar. The individual works, including momentary com-binations of the visual, the verbal and the performing arts, will be displayed everywhere – in the streets, in parks, along highways, in labs, in offices, planes and cars, in schools and colleges, supermarkets and department stores, on the sides of buildings, in canals and occasionally on the air rights over bridges. The museum's collections and commissioned works will be constantly moving. A staggering array of travelling exhibitions will make the Logistics Officer of the Sixth Fleet look like the booking agent of a bad Broadway show com-pared to the registrar of a major modern museum. Most im-portantly, the museum will be directing the use of its collections rather than the collections determining the direc-tion of the museum.[15]

Mr Hightower believes, and a great many people in all coun-

tries would agree with him, that the most important educational task our twentieth-century society has to face is the
control and improvement of the environment in which we live
and work. By confining our campaigns to institutions, we have
undermined our ability to influence the situation. 'We are', he
says, 'losing the battle to remind ourselves of just how critical
the visual quality of our environment really is.'

> Museums can no longer afford to be a quiet corner on a
> Sunday afternoon. Art is the synthesis of man's ability to see.
> Through art, all forms of art, museums must take a leading
> role in helping us to perceive and respect – or be outraged at
> – our surroundings. Public education has not demonstrated
> it is aware that the battle for the ability to see is impossible,
> much less desperate. Despite the fact that we are bombarded
> daily by sight communication, the curriculum of many
> of our schools does not include any use of visual dis-
> crimination. Museums must take the lead. They can do
> so by design or they can do so by default. Neither artist
> nor public will allow their attention to be indifferent.
> The artist's role in the conspiracy against maintaining a
> nineteenth-century museum is becoming as intense as
> the public's.[16]

If museums are in the communication business, as they
purport to be, it is worth enquiring what is, in fact, being
communicated? It may, of course, be a love of museums
for their own sake. There is nothing disreputable about
this. One can enjoy cathedrals without admiring bishops
or cemeteries without being dead. It is not necessary to be
a botanist in order to derive great pleasure from strolling
round the glasshouses at Kew. The authorities who run
cathedrals, cemeteries or glasshouses may have fairly precise ideas as to what they are trying to accomplish, but
the people who visit these places may simply like being
there. The atmosphere is agreeable to them.

Mrs Shann, the eldest daughter of the great Victorian director of the British Museum, Sir William Henry Flower, never became a doctor or a zoologist, yet she recalled with enormous
pleasure one particular museum where she spent a good deal of
time as a little girl.

When we were small, and very happy and energetic [she remembered] the Museum of the College of Surgeons was a most familiar place to us, as we lived in the house next door, and my father used to enter it at all hours, and often take us with him. We delighted in these visits, and had our special favourites among the exhibits. The most exciting were the tall skeleton of the Irish giant, and that of the little Polish dwarf with her tiny shoe and thimble, which had long been among the treasures of the collection. Another great object of our admiration was the remains of the Siberian Mammoth, with its real skin and hair, and the monkeys. These on certain wet half-holidays we were allowed to have out to play with instead of a doll, whilst we paid and received visits from and in our respective 'houses' under the big whale or the giant sloth, which still are conspicuous and formidable figures in the collection. I always recall the odour of fresh paint and varnish (on the cases and stands) and the peculiar smell of the carefully prepared and whitened bones. Occasionally we were allowed the excitement of a good run round in the upper galleries 'all among the bottles'. One of the strongest desires of my childhood was to be allowed to spend a night in the Museum.[17]

The Museum of the College of Surgeons was undoubtedly capable of giving great pleasure to one small child, but this is probably not the same thing as saying that it was either a good or a successful museum, since it was not designed to give pleasure to small children. From the point of view of the College, Mrs Shann was, one might say, a bonus. But can one be successful only by planning to be successful? Must everything good be deliberate? Is nothing to be left to chance and individual whim?

These questions and a number of others were looked at during a seminar held in 1967 at the Museum of the City of New York. Its proceedings were subsequently published under the title, *Exploration of the ways, means and values of Museum Communication with the Viewing Public*.[18] The protagonists were Harley W. Parker, of the Royal Ontario Museum, Toronto, and Dr Marshall McLuhan. Both of them disagreed strongly with nearly every one of the ideas cherished by the museum establishment.

One could set out their major statements as a Catalogue of

Notions guaranteed to make the Director of the British Museum reach for his gun. They do not need to be set out or interpreted in any particular order. The effect is cumulative.

> *Dr McLuhan* It came as a great shock, thirty or thirty-five years ago, to discover that the same words spoken to two different people mean quite different things. There is a book called *Seven Types of Ambiguity*. To the literary community, in 1932, when this book came out, it was a great shock to discover that the most clear and simple expressions have totally different meanings to different people when written or printed. Words don't mean the same thing to any two people, and they shouldn't. It is our job to make sense. Sense isn't something that should be stuffed down your throat. It's something you have to 'make' on your own. . . You know, the whole theory of communication considers it as the transfer of a certain item to a certain area intact. That's for the legal profession, and they're not doing so well. They're having plenty of trouble.[19]

> *Mr Parker* If we relate this to the simple facts of the difference between, let's say, tactile, kinetic and Old World as opposed to the visual world – as Leonardo da Vinci said, 'Seeing is believing' – but the whole quotation is 'Seeing is believing but to touch them is the word of God'. If we begin to extrapolate this kind of idea into the museum world, it raises this factor – that the audience has changed so radically in the last thirty years since the War. I don't think that in the whole history of man there has been such a sudden change in sensibility. So my own position, in terms of museums, is this: certainly, concern with artifacts is a very necessary thing, this is the curatorial job, the curatorial function; but it seems to me that with this tremendous change in audience we must have people within museums who are concerned with audience – audience reaction. We must get feedback, we must find out how to present these artifacts which we are looking after so carefully.[20]

> *Dr McLuhan* You remember the scandal that the sculptures of Moore created when they went to Germany and the audience was told not to lay a hand on them? The idea that

sculpture should not be touched seemed utter heresy to the Germans.

Mr Parker I even encountered this in the Royal Imperial Museum, where there is a fossil tree which was about 500 million years old. It was on display and there was a small boy standing there running his fingers over it, and the guard came along and said, 'Don't touch'. It was around for 500 million years and they would not let him touch it.

Dr McLuhan The theme of touch which is so basic now with the TV generation. . . . They, having been X-rayed by the TV image from early childhood, now feel the need of handling all things in depth. The old pictorial, external look at things will not serve. But another peculiarity about touch is this: granted that there is the natural human desire to touch, the fact that touch creates an interval involves the audience very much more, the interval has to be closed. When you create an interval you have to close it and it is the closing of the interval that creates participation and rhythm.[21]

Mr Parker Museums of course in the past have tended – museum curators tend today – to also write a story line and then use the artifacts to illustrate it. In fact, if they were writing a book they would do exactly the same thing, except that in this case the artifacts would be photographed and used as illustrations, but there is no essential difference. In other words they think of a museum as a book.

Dr McLuhan That is one of the peculiarities, and nobody needs to be told this, in a way, about EXPO 67. It is perhaps the first world fair which had no story line whatever. It was just a mosaic of discontinuous items in which people took an immense satisfaction precisely *because* they weren't being told anything about the overall pattern or shape of it, but they were free to discover and participate and involve themselves in the total overall thing. The result was also that they never got fatigued. I remember as a youngster being familiar with a phrase, which I may have invented, 'that museum feeling', a kind of claustrophobia and exhaustion which settles upon you as soon as you get inside those straightened avenues and alleyways. Once

you move into a world of continuous, connected space –
visual space – you quickly discover exhaustion setting in,
because there is no means of participation.[22]

Dr McLuhan You see, I have watched people in museums for
many years and it is rather interesting, both in Europe and
America. You find a person will walk up to an object and
look at it casually, read the label, give it a cursory glance,
and walk on. They have not really looked at anything, because they are data-oriented and they figure that now
they've got the answer to that and they know it is tenth-
century this or that, so they walk away from it. So the idea
of setting up a gallery which just asks questions is going to
force people to look at that or touch it if possible but at any
rate look at it.[23]

One gets the message without too much difficulty. Impressions,
participation, rhythm, audience reaction, whatever these
things may mean, are good. The story-line, the label, words, a
wish to instruct, are bad.

It is always possible, of course, that if and when the majority
of the world's museums are of the type recommended by Mr
Parker and Dr McLuhan, a new kind of quiet, orderly, restful
museum will arise to meet the needs of the minority who are
deafened, blinded and exhausted by the new-style attempts to
make museums meaningful.

Dr McLuhan's ideas are fashionable, which is another way
of saying that at some time in the possibly not very distant
future they will cease to be fashionable. Many of yesterday's
bold museum experiments already seem faded, quaint or
absurd, although they were daring and useful in their time.
Even Artur Hazelius, the creator of Skansen and the originator
of the concept of the open-air museum, has been much criticised for being over-interested in systematisation. The motor-
car, wrote Bo Lagercrantz in 1964, has made the Skansen idea
obsolete. Buildings no longer have to be brought to people.
People can go to buildings. There is no need for more open-air
museums, he says. We should preserve the old buildings *in situ*.
'The removal of entire buildings does too much violence to their
past.'[24]

What Mr Lagercrantz appears to overlook is that the demo-

lition of old buildings, to make way for office-blocks, motor-
ways and reservoirs, does even more violence to their past.
Without open-air museums, a large number of interesting
buildings would have vanished long ago. And, very sadly or
reprehensibly, the public continues to like open-air museums.
The two established in Britain recently, Beamish, in the North-
East, and Ironbridge, in the West Midlands, are both proving
immensely popular with visitors. Mr Lagercrantz was, of
course, writing in the days of cheap petrol, when it was a relatively simple matter to visit a windmill here and a
wheelwright's shop there. Today, this is an expensive matter
and it is probable that people will be increasingly grateful for
the opportunity which the open-air museum provides to make a
single journey yield a rich return.

There are, in any case, things which can be done at a central-
ised open-air museum which are much more difficult to achieve
elsewhere. At Beamish, for instance, the aim is to provide a
range of what are called 'historic experiences'. A pitman's cot-
tage, explains the Director

> could give girls an opportunity to try baking bread in the
> coal-fired oven, letting the dough rise in front of the fire. Or
> washday could be experienced, heating water in the side
> boiler and using a posser and mangle.

Among the other experiences offered are 'the opportunity to use
a 1920s classroom, with uncomfortable long bench-seated
desks, old blackboard, inkwells and abacus' and, eventually,
pit-sawing, butter and cheese-making, candle-making and
rope-making. These activities demand quite a lot of planning
and supervision, which are much more practicable if they can
be carried on at one site. Whether they would meet Dr
McLuhan's definition of participation is difficult to say.

What are loosely called 'open-air museums' are very varied.
Such a museum may be wholly an assemblage of buildings
brought from elsewhere, it may be partly composed of buildings on their original site and partly of imported material, it
may contain, among its exhibits, a high proportion of items
which are not buildings at all.

At Kinderdijk, in the Netherlands, for example, the seventeen windmills, of different types and dating from the eight-

eenth and nineteenth centuries, undoubtedly constitute an open-air museum (see Plate 14). They were built to form an integrated pumping unit, for drainage purposes, and, although they have long since been replaced by electric pumps so far as work is concerned, they are kept in good condition, as a landscape feature which tourists in particular like to see, and as a set of technological monuments.

The little nineteenth-century milk-processing factory at Ølgod, West Jutland, stands, as a museum, in the middle of what is still an important dairying region. One can perfectly logically regard the factory in its context, the whole area in fact, as what the French call an 'eco-museum'. The eco-museum can properly include trees, plants, animals, a factory, a farm, cottages, a road, a railway tunnel – anything which happens to be there at the moment when one decides to study it. It could be defined as a piece of landscape or townscape with all its belongings. To apply the word 'museum' to such an unstable entity, even in the compound 'eco-museum' might be considered by some purists to be stretching a definition a little far, since most of the museum's collections must inevitably be of a very impermanent character and the museum itself does not own the area it exists to serve. Yet, if one of the earliest eco-museums, the Museum of Man and Industry at Le Creusot, in France, is any guide, the existence of the museum, with its central headquarters building – a fine eighteenth-century château – and its active friends and supporters throughout the substantial area of Burgundy which the museum covers, undoubtedly creates a greatly increased historical and social awareness among local people. This, in turn, leads to an understanding of the value of preserving familiar objects, large and small, and in this way the museum's 'collections' may well become a little more permanent each year. The headquarters, in any case, acts as a repository right from the beginning for material which would otherwise be lost. In present circumstances, when participation is the order of the day and when money for conventional museums is hard to come by, the attractions of the eco-museum are very great; and it would be surprising if there were not to be a considerable amount of experiment and development in this direction.

It is perfectly possible and reasonable to have a museum

within a museum. The National Parks in a number of countries do precisely this. The Park itself is a museum of trees and plants and wild-life, and as its core there is an explanatory museum, or visitor centre. The Americans and Canadians have been particularly successful at this. The Dinosaur Provincial Park, near Patricia, Alberta, for instance, is famous for the dinosaur skeletons which have been found there, but it is also a pleasant place in its own right, visited by large numbers of holiday-makers during the summer months. It would be an exaggeration, perhaps, to say that the dinosaurs are felt to be of less importance than the scenery, but one could fairly feel that each season's visitors contain relatively few people with a professional or specialist interest in dinosaurs. The small site-museum can therefore content itself with showing the visitors some fossilised skeletons of dinosaurs and with giving them some basic information about how the discoveries were made. This is an interest-creation, not a scientific museum, and a simple style of presentation is perfectly in place.

The value that can be obtained by keeping material on its original site can be very great, and such a policy often turns out to be the most economical, as well as the most effective. This is well illustrated by two widely separated examples, one in Hungary and the other in the Irish Republic.

At Pápa, not far from Budapest, a small factory for dyeing cloth was established in 1786 by a family which had migrated from Saxony. This indigo dye-house continued to operate until after the 1939–45 war. It has now been restored and preserved, complete with all its machinery and equipment, as the museum of an industry which was once of considerable importance in several European countries. The cost of converting the dye-house into a museum was very small and the effect is much greater than could possibly have been obtained, even with the most skilful treatment, by dismantling the equipment and moving it to an existing museum. So often these uprooted work-places lose all their atmosphere when they are transferred else-where. In the museum at Furtwangen, in the Black Forest, for example, there is a reconstruction of a clockmaker's work-shop, containing original tools and furniture. It is so clean and orderly as to be unconvincing, charming, beautifully preserved and dead – a boudoir of a workshop. One finds it difficult to believe that real work was ever carried on in such a place.

The College at Maynooth, not far from Dublin, has in its museum some of the electrical equipment invented and made during the 1839s by the Rev. Dr Callan, who was a member of the staff of this large and famous seminary. One item is an electro-magnet nearly seven feet high, which had a lifting capacity of several tons, with the repeater used by Callan to interrupt the primary current. He constructed this device from the escapement mechanism of an old grandfather clock. Also preserved is Callan's medium-sized coil, the secondary winding of which consisted of ten miles of fine iron wire – not easy to obtain in the 1830s – insulated with a mixture of beeswax and gutta-percha. The layers were separated by sheets of paper soaked in the same insulating mixture.

Dr Callan's apparatus would certainly be seen by more people each year in a museum – the great argument of the centralisers – than in a provincial seminary. But a good deal would have been lost by moving it. Much of its interest rests in the fact that it was designed and made by a seminary priest in his spare time and with his own hands. To see it at Maynooth, where it was created, with the college buildings much as they were when Callan was there, is to understand it in its proper and most meaningful context. The imagination does not have to work so hard at Maynooth as it would in Dublin.

One type of museum rides the ideological and financial storms with remarkable ease and becomes steadily more popular each year. This is the museum known to the trade as the historic house museum.[25] There are two broad categories, which often overlap – the house which is interesting for its architecture and its furnishings and the house which has at some time been the home of a famous person. Historic house museums are immune to fashion. They are essentially survivals from the past and they make their impact by their honesty and by their ability to preserve the atmosphere of the period when they were functioning units. Unless the management is very incompetent, they are never cluttered up with exhibition cases or other irrelevant impedimenta. They contain only what belonged to them, or could have belonged to them, when they were in use. They have no lighting or sound effects, and a minimum of labelling, and their most important characteristic is that they are small and simple enough to prevent the visitor from getting tired or feeling hopelessly ignorant. They are museums in which one feels safe.

It is not easy to say the same about the so-called 'objective' museum or exhibition style, which was first seen, on a thorough-going scale, at Hartford, Connecticut, in 1934. This conception of a museum as a technological exercise produced the Essen Museum in the Ruhr, and the extension of the Germanisches Museum, in Nürnberg, both of which were completed in 1950. The style has been defined, following Le Corbusier, as 'a machine for presenting works of art'.[26] Paintings are taken out of their frames, hung free in space or on very light free-standing frames, sculptures are placed on transparent ramps or pedestals, to give them the impression of floating in the air. The aim is to make the surroundings of each exhibit entirely neutral, so that the object is viewed in its own right, with no associations of any kind. Given such treatment, even familiar works change their character completely. They are naked prisoners in empty cells, with nothing to confuse the viewer, and, equally, nothing to help him.

How much help, in fact, does the museum visitor need or want? It is interesting to observe the difference in the views held about this, by the curators of most museums on the one hand and most historic houses on the other. In museums, the attendants are essentially policemen. It is rare for them to offer information or to be asked for it. In historic houses, on the other hand, the attendants – very often there is only one – tend to be guides as well. They are less forbidding and appear to be more knowledgeable, although this is occasionally an illusion. In one of the most famous of the English country houses open to the public, the writer remembers being told by the guide-attendant, concerning a German woodcarving, that the Saint shown by the side of a blazing house was the patron saint of horses. The typescript supplied by the owners, the National Trust, had contained an unfortunate typing error, which common sense had failed to correct.

Museums get, to a large extent, what they pay for, and for attendants they have always paid very little. During her travels round Europe and America in the early part of the present century, Margaret Talbot Jackson took a careful look at the calibre of the staff:

> The European museum, as part of the State government, is manned by returned soldiers, men who through long service to the State have acquired respect and veneration for public property that makes them reliable and dependable. These men, once they obtain a position, are there for life unless something unforeseen happens. In America no man takes any such position with the intention of staying in it long – only until he can find something better.[27]

Courtesy was necessary – 'the museums have lost many friends through the rudeness of the custodians' – and intelligence of a sort was useful, 'although just where it is desirable and where it becomes objectionable is the question. A too garrulous custodian who babbles fairy tales about the objects in his charge is offensive, but a certain amount of knowledge of all the collections of the museum and a little accurate information about the objects directly in his charge is very desirable.'[28]

The pay of museum employees has been notoriously and scandalously low for as long as there have been museums. 'I have before me', Sir William Henry Flower told the Museums Association in 1893 in his Presidential Address, 'some recent advertisements

> The curator of the Museum of the Philosophical and Literary Society of one of the largest and most flourishing of our manufacturing cities is offered £125 a year for his services. In another town, smaller and less wealthy, it is true, 'a resident curator, metereological observer, and caretaker, is wanted for the museum and library buildings, at a salary of £50 per annum, with rooms, coal and gas. Applicants are to state age and scientific qualifications.'[29]

It would have been better, he believed, if many museums had never been founded, since they had neither the money nor the will to pay their staff properly. In such cases 'a grievously undersalaried and consequently uneducated individual is expected to keep in order, to clean, dust, arrange, name and display in a manner which will contribute to the advancement of scientific knowledge, collections ranging in extent over almost every branch of human learning, from the contents of an ancient British barrow to the last discovered bird of paradise from New Guinea'.[30]

It would not be accurate to say that the staff of at least the major museums throughout the world are quite as badly paid now, in relation to other professions, as they were in the 1890s. What is more commonly the case is that, in order to be able to empire-build within an inadequate budget, a museum director will acquire as many professional staff as he decently can and then find himself without the funds to employ sufficient technicians and secretaries to allow the professionals to do their work properly. In London, the number of secretaries at, for example, the Science Museum would probably come as a considerable shock to most people outside the museum world.

Given this situation, it is hardly surprising that museums do not change their exhibitions as often as they might like to or that visitor surveys are so frequently regarded as an impossible luxury.

5
MUSEUMS IN THE MARKET RESEARCH AGE

In 1961 Duncan F. Cameron and D. S. Abbey took stock of what had so far been accomplished by research into the character, habits and wishes of visitors to museums. Their conclusions were not encouraging. 'For over thirty years now,' they wrote,

> museum workers in North America have been using scientific methods in the study of museum audiences. Unknowing visitors have been tracked through galleries by observers armed with stop-watch and clip-board. Thousands have been accosted by interviewers at the turnstiles, in the exhibit halls and in the street. Yet in spite of these many and varied endeavors, the useful knowledge accumulated is slight, and the value of such investigations remains a matter of diverse opinion in the museum profession.[1]

The main reason, they believed, for the widespread unwillingness, if not refusal, to accept visitor research as a normal, useful professional tool was that it had been, by modern standards, poorly done. It is not absolutely clear what they had in mind by this. 'Poorly done' can mean either that the surveys were, in market research terms, statistically inadequate, that the sampling method was unsatisfactory, that the questions were badly phrased or simply that the wrong questions were asked. Any of these weaknesses is sufficient to damn a survey in the eyes of those who earn their living in the market research field. But 'poorly done' could, and probably does, imply something quite different, that the whole venture is misguided in some way, that the attempt to quantify people's reactions to museums or to museum displays distorts or even falsifies their real response to what is presented to them. Many museum curators would say, and indeed have said to the present author, that they believe they can learn as much by wandering round with their ears and eyes open as by commissioning an expensive, scientifically planned research operation. Some museums make a practice of compiling a running list of remarks overheard in their galleries. Cumulatively, this can be a valuable management tool, always assuming that the staff have the skill, imagination and objectivity to interpret what they hear. Visitors' remarks can be a useful supplement to scientifically planned research, but it is helpful to know roughly what kind of person is being reported. Is it a man or a woman, young or elderly? Has anything been observed of the person's behaviour in the museum, any clue to suggest interest or lack of interest?

The Guggenheim Foundation has assembled a large number of unsolicited comments made by visitors to the 10th anniversary exhibition of the Museum of Non-Objective Painting in New York.[2] These, it should be emphasised, are not overheard remarks. They are thoughts put down on paper after visiting the museum and it is difficult to believe that the same people would have expressed themselves in exactly this way if they had been talking instead of writing. Allowing for the possibility that some selection may have been made – we are not told if we have a random sample of comments – these visitors appear to take themselves very seriously indeed and to be well soaked in psychological jargon, which is, of course, not uncommon in the United States. One has no clear picture of the man or woman who wrote: 'This is the only museum I have ever seen which makes me feel that it is sincerely interested in furthering the growth and deepening the insight of all creative endeavors. This museum really serves humanity; I wish there were more like it.'

'The paintings of Bauer', declared one enthusiast, 'are messages of intimations of immortality, of man's communing with spatial profundity.' Other visitors went further, and testified to the extent to which the exhibition, not unlike a working patent medicine, had transformed their lives.

I had lived in France for years, then everything was lost. I came to America a broken person. I walked around as if a great weight were on my shoulders. One day someone showed me some prints from the non-objective museum, and I came to see the paintings. Somehow each visit brought subtle changes. I was able to go about building up my life again. People who had not seen me since my arrival hardly recognised me. I felt thirty years of difference in my face. Now I walked as if on air. Non-objectivity has caused this miracle for me.[3]

It is an ungenerous and blinkered definition of feedback which would not include the kind of comments quoted above. One has to remember, however, that there is now a considerable body of highly-trained specialists, especially in the United States, which earns its living from the application of 'scientific methods', and, this being so, it would be unreasonable to expect mere eavesdropping, conversation and intuition, all of which are free, to have a very high prestige, any more than country walks are popular with those professionally involved in the leisure industries. With this proviso, one can record that Mr Cameron and Mr Abbey believe that museums should be interested in feedback. 'Periodic surveys of small samples of visitors, before and after their visits to the galleries, using a standard questionnaire with carefully worded questions, could keep the museum staff informed of the appeal of the exhibits, and the changes in interests.'[4] Museums are, in other words, recommended to follow normal commercial procedures.

The first aspect of museums to receive serious attention from the behavioural scientists was the power of the exhibits, or of certain exhibits to seize and hold a visitor's attention. In his book, *The Behavior of the Museum Visitor*, which Edward S. Robinson wrote for the American Association of Museums in 1928, it was revealed that, on the average, people looked at pictures for nine seconds in large museums and for twelve to fifteen seconds in small museums. The reason was supposed to be the greater number of distractions – Mr Robinson used the more dignified phrase, 'calls on attention' – in the larger establishment. The implication was clearly that the longer a person looked at a picture, the more successfully a museum was doing its job.

In 1939 another American observer, Laurence Vail Coleman,

castigated museum visitors for their casual, unmethodical habits.

> Most visitors do not read their labels with any thoroughness. There are, to be sure, exceptional people who will read and transcribe even a very long label, and other sports of nature who will inspect every label in a room; but such cases are rare. All too many visitors pick up only a word here and a sentence there, and let it go at that. Sustained reading on foot is not induced as a habit by other activities of life, and no other institution besides the museum calls upon people to learn standing up.[5]

This notion that people learn better sitting down than standing up is curious. What Mr Coleman means is that, at the time at which he was writing, learning was chiefly associated with school or college, and school or college meant sitting down at a desk with a book. Yet, even in 1939, a great deal of learning and intellectual work went on in laboratories of one kind and another, where it was perfectly normal to stand up, and in all periods it has been rare for painters and sculptors to work except on their feet. It is, in any case, significant that Mr Coleman uses the word 'learn'. For him, a museum is essentially a place where one learns, not where one is *stimulated* to learn or where one modifies one's attitudes. It is an intellectual place, where the reading of labels is one of the most important tasks the visitor has to perform.

Mr Coleman was able to report progress with labels.

> In the past few years a start has been made at experimental study of labeling to find out how the visitor reads and what can be done about it. As might be expected this points to the superior chances a short label has of being looked at, and finds that particularities are more acceptable than a systematic development of ideas in the text. This suggests that science museums might do well to consider the art museum's plan of labeling and provide exhibit leaflets in support of fragmentary labels.[6]

What this amounts to is a system of two-level signposting and information, brief captions for people who want no more than that and leaflets for people who are interested in digging deeper. Shortly before Mr Coleman's book appeared, Mildred C. B. Porter had been watching visitors at the Peabody Museum of Natural History. She had discovered that guide leaflets persuaded a visitor to stay longer in the Museum, made him look at more exhibits and read more labels.[7]

We have already mentioned the well-known definition of an educational museum produced by G. Browne Goode in 1895, when he was in charge of the United States National Museum: 'An efficient educational museum may be described as a collection of instructive labels, each illustrated by a well-selected specimen.' Much less attention has been paid to Goode's qualifying statement, that the merit of a label 'depends much more on what you leave out than on what you put in'. In an age that was much given to wordiness, and that had an extraordinary belief in the appeal of facts, Goode's advice mostly fell on deaf ears. Few museums attached any value to his warning that a label 'may contain a vast amount of exact and valuable information, and yet, by reason of faulty literary and typographical arrangement, have as little significance and value as a piece of blank paper.'

When George Weiner went to the Smithsonian Institution in the early 1960s as Supervisory Exhibits Editor he found that, despite Goode's missionary activities sixty-eight years earlier, the labels were too long and typographically poor. They were not performing their prime duty of answering 'at least the initial questions that a reasonably curious visitor might be disposed to ask'.[8] Mr Weiner was a strong believer in labels. Nothing better, he felt, had ever been invented. 'Guidebooks or audio systems are useful informational aids, but they cannot reach a fraction of the audience that labels can. Therefore labels become virtually the only means by which the majority of viewers are able to derive any benefit whatsoever from a museum.'[9]

The National Gallery of Art in Washington conducted an experiment[10] during the 1960s to test the effectiveness of the free interpretation leaflets for its pictures. A group of fifteen undergraduates was asked to evaluate the entries on the leaflet. 'Names, symbols and subject-matter characterize the "iconographic" sentence. Dates, periods and stylistic characteristics relate to "art-historical" sentences', says the report, 'which may or may not relate to specific elements pointed out in the painting. The "esthetic" sentence points to elements in the painting itself.'

For Franz Hals' painting, *A Young Man in a Large Hat,* the leaflet says

Hals, a generation older than Rembrandt, is one of the pioneers of Dutch painting. His great achievement was his ability to record the momentary expressions and spontaneous gestures of his subjects with bold and rapid brush strokes. The unknown subject of this study was probably a gay blade in his native city of Harlem.

This is a fair example of the general tone and level of the leaflets.

In the analysis of the sentences selected as being most helpful, 3 per cent were found to be iconographic, 55 per cent art-historical, and 42 per cent aesthetic. When, however, the questioning was narrowed down, to find the greatest measure of agreement as to which sentences were the most helpful, the aesthetic won. The undergraduates, whose opinions may or may not have represented those of the general public, favoured such information as 'Turner has transformed this scene of grimy toil into a dreamlike vision by flooding the seascape with the light of glowing torches and a harvest moon.'

Few institutions have investigated their visitors as continuously and as thoroughly as the Milwaukee Public Museum. In 1952–53 it organised a survey to discover the basic facts about visitors to the Museum, where they came from, their age, sex, educational background, income group. However, they decided there was more to a museum visitor than his sex and his income group – 'finding out his reaction to and how well he understood an exhibit is a different problem.'[11] To avoid making gross misjudgements, the Milwaukee Museum has used test exhibits, as a guide to the public's taste, knowledge and ability to assimilate information. The experimental exhibit is

of a conceptual nature – Culture versus Environment. By

employing the personal interview technique, a controlled statistical analysis is being made of visitor response to a series of variations on this item; that is, extensive versus minimal labelling, many specimens versus few specimens, color variations versus monotone presentation. In this study we hope to determine the relative effectiveness of the three basic display techniques before we use them singly or in combination in our new exhibit hall.[12]

An enquiry carried out by the Milwaukee Museum in 1965 to test display techniques for an anthropological exhibit used a two-page questionnaire which is reproduced as Appendix II. The experiment was mainly concerned with discovering which background colours were most effective, but what was revealed by the questionnaire contained information of more fundamental importance. It was clear, firstly, that the visitors to the museum were 'better educated and more demanding than we realise',[13] and secondly that the style of display was too bare and slender. Milwaukee learnt the lesson.

> Museum exhibit designers may find it advisable to return to well-filled displays and above all to de-emphasize tricky or extraneous 'art work' in case exhibits. That is not to say that we advocate displays which are truly overcrowded; instead, we recommend some sort of compromise between open storage and the ultra-selective exhibits which are the trend today.[14]

This is a way of saying either that museum visitors are disappointingly conservative, or that, left to themselves, museum designers would be designing primarily for themselves and their professional colleagues, not for the public. But it is surely right to be adventurous and to go on experimenting, no matter how much discouragement there may be from time to time. The museum that never has any new ideas is unworthy to stay in business. The controversy really centres around whether museum display is an art or a science. Few of those professionally engaged would want to take the art out of exhibit design and none would deny that people can be attracted by ingenious and dramatic effects. One well-known American designer, Harris T. Shettel, has firmly and publicly rejected[15] the yardstick which says that if Exhibit A attracts more people than Exhibit B, then Exhibit A is better than Exhibit B, mainly because the excessive use of what he calls 'attention-getting techniques' may actually reduce the educational value of the exhibit.

'Given', he says, 'X dollars to spend on an exhibit, the temptation to use them for the "sizzle" rather than the steak may be difficult to resist. However, this situation is not likely to improve as long as those working in the field are content to equate popularity and effectiveness.'[16] He does, even so, believe that exhibit design is to some extent a science and that in all forms of communication 'improved statements of intended objectives and evaluation instruments based on these objectives are of primary importance.'

Mr Shettel has devised what he calls an 'exhibit effectiveness rating scale' for the use of museum staff. It asks questions of this type:

1 Not all subject matter lends itself to the exhibit medium. How suitable is this subject matter for exhibit presentation?

Excellent   Good   Fair   Poor

WHY? ————————————————————————————

(*NOTE: The above format was repeated for each item on the scale.*)

2 How would you rate the following in terms of visitor ease of viewing?
   a. The exhibit's distance from the visitor
   b. Its physical layout (height of exhibit; amount of material displayed; placement and arrangement of material within the exhibit)
3 How would you rate this exhibit on its appropriate use of color?
4 How would you rate the main title of this exhibit from the standpoint of:
   a. Wording-content
   b. Design

and so on. Another American, Dillon Ripley, has proposed[17] breaking away from the questionnaire system altogether and replacing it by button-pushing. People would not be told or

even asked to press the buttons. They would do so of their own
accord, as part of the museum game. The information would be
recorded on tape and Dr Ripley believes that a study of it

> might give us a clue to why people in a museum liked round
> objects or square objects, stuffed elephants or steam engines,
> paneled rooms or Eskimo igloos complete with Eskimo mani-
> kins. We might find out not only why people react to things in
> a certain way, but what these reactions stem from, and if in-
> terest has been created or is capable of being created by the
> very reaction itself.

The dangers inherent in the button-pushing approach were
foreseen many years ago by the English novelist, Aldous
Huxley. His reaction-testing cinema had each seat equipped
with a control to be turned left or right continuously during the
progress of the film they had been brought to see. Turned one
way, the knob indicated varying degrees of pleasure; turned the
other, distaste. These movements were fed into a central regis-
tering system which, in its turn, was connected with a shot-by-
shot running order of the film. Before each film was finally re-
leased to the public, everything the audience had disliked was
removed from it. The result, inevitably, was a film which
nobody wanted to see. The designers of this particular piece of
research had entirely failed to grasp the important truth that
pleasure and pain always co-exist. One enjoys something only
within the context of other things that one hates or fears.

It is, in any case, very doubtful if Dr Ripley's buttons would
give visitors an opportunity to say if they were black or white, a
very important detail in any piece of research in America. The
present writer has never seen a questionnaire in which this was
asked – it would almost certainly cause difficulties under the
race discrimination laws – yet it is perfectly well known that
black people and white people can react very differently to the
same exhibit. At a conference held in Washington in 1972, a
black delegate told the audience that the Smithsonian was a
white man's museum. Everything in it was made by white men,
mostly for other white men. Any black man who went there felt
an outsider as soon as he entered the doors. Yet the most casual
glance reveals that there are always black people among the
visitors. Are they having different thoughts from the white visi-

tors? The Smithsonian has no idea. It has never tried to find out. It probably dare not make the attempt.

During the past twenty-five years there is no doubt that the Americans have gone a very long way ahead of any other country, both in carrying out research among their visitors and in attaching value to the results. America is a country in which market research is rated very highly, even by the churches. Even so, many museums in other parts of the world have carried out surveys from time to time, either in connexion with particular projects, or to check up on what visitors thought of the museum as a whole. The largest and most important of these surveys was undertaken by the Ulster Museum in 1967, as a necessary prelude to its major extension and reshaping programme, and the results published in the *Museums Journal* the following year.[18]

In his introduction to this report, the author, Philip S. Doughty, drew attention to the extent to which Britain had neglected visitor surveys. 'It is a remarkable fact', he observed

> that until this decade there was not a single British museum with published results of surveys to discover who its visitors were, how effective its displays were, what the public liked and disliked. Even now only one other museum has done this. In its affected self-esteem the profession has not lost touch with its public – it simply never found it, or even attempted to. In a conference devoted entirely to public relations not a single objectively established fact about the public was employed in any paper. If this arrogance continues it is difficult to see how museums can find their place in society or serve a useful purpose as display centres.

The Ulster Museum survey was conducted on five July weekdays, Monday, Tuesday and Friday of one week and Monday and Tuesday of the following week. On these days, every visitor to the museum, apart from children below the age of seven, was asked to complete a questionnaire and about 50 per cent did so. The questionnaire aimed at discovering basic personal details (age, sex, place of residence, occupation) and then passed into details connected more specifically with the Museum – had they been there before, how long had they spent in the Museum, why had they come. For the last question, there were five possibilities – to see the whole museum, to have something identified, to make an enquiry, to see a special exhibit, to pass the time. They were also asked which parts of the Museum they had visited, which they liked best and least, how they had travelled to the Museum, whether they had ever patronised any of its activities, such as film shows, and what improvements they would like to see.

The survey, although undoubtedly useful, was not without certain humorous features. As a way of discovering how much of the museum people had seen, a selection of exhibits, distributed around the galleries, was given. Any item on the list that had been looked at was to be ticked. Included on the list was a wholly fictitious item, which did not exist at all. A considerable number of people ticked it, a fact which drew from Mr Doughty the somewhat straightlaced response that 'this does underline the lax approach of the public to museum exhibits'.

But, whatever the public may have thought about the exhibits at the Ulster Museum, the survey left no doubt that the physical amenities were not well regarded. 'Staircases are barriers, lifts are not clearly marked, seats are uncomfortable, and only discovered by diligent search, and there are no facilities for refreshment.' Failings of this kind are not difficult to correct, and since this report was published, many of them have in fact been remedied. More serious, however, in the view of the Museum's administration, was the revelation that visitors did not represent a cross-section of the adult public. There was, it appeared, a tendency to see museum visiting as 'a juvenile pastime', which was felt to be a cause for concern. On the other hand, Philip Doughty, who was presumably speaking for the Museum as well as himself, was convinced that it was wrong to go too far in the direction of the 'consumer-oriented' museum, because such a policy, aimed at pleasing the public at all costs, would mean starving the other branches of the museum's work of funds.[19]

This view is debatable. In 1955, Dr D. B. Harden gave his opinion[20] that, for most people, a museum was essentially a place of entertainment and amusement. His views were echoed in 1969, after the publication of Doughty's report by C. A. Sizer, who criticised the deductions made from it, and declared that 'the more museums try to educate the public, the more resistance they will encounter'.[21] He went on to say that 'the general public wants its money's worth (even if it does not pay for admission) and perhaps regards museums as another type of trade fair, agricultural show or stately home'. It is curious to find museums still being placed, in the professional mind, in one self-contained box, with trade fairs, agricultural shows and stately homes in another. Very few members of the general public think in this way and in the Communist countries, for instance, the convention of making a sharp distinction between museums and exhibitions has been officially much weakened, if not abolished. At both the Russian and Chinese ends of the Communist spectrum the view is firmly held that all displays – it is wisest to use a neutral word – should serve the overall purpose of education and that in order to achieve this it is entirely proper to mix old with new and to apply whatever techniques may seem likely to work.

A good example of this is the Exhibition of Economic Achievements, on the outskirts of Moscow. To put the matter in British terms, here, on a large, open site, are blended the Empire Exhibition, held at Wembley in 1923 and 1924, the Science Museum, the Bath and West Show, the Radio Show and Battersea Gardens. A huge and splendidly arranged collection illustrates the history of Soviet rocketry and space exploration; physics and plant-breeding have large buildings of their own; demonstration orchards mingle with a cinema-in-the-round and a Pavilion of the Fur Industry. Nobody seems to bother their heads in the least about such theological arguments as whether an agricultural show should be on speaking terms with a science museum. The public clearly likes this kind of variety and it gets it.

Another strange feature of both Doughty's and Sizer's reports is their apparent blindness to the existence of the escalator. Stairs, they both agree, are a terrible barrier. But, for a very long time now, toiling up stairs has been quite unnecessary. The museum which is bothered about the problem has only to install escalators to see the barrier disappear. At the Central Lenin Museum in Moscow, for example, there are quite as many visitors on the first and second floors as on the ground floor, since the building – an old building – has been generously equipped with escalators.

Another weakness in the Ulster Museum Survey, and indeed in most other surveys, is that it was concerned only with people who were actually visiting the museum. It made no attempt to discover the views of the public as a whole, that is, of both visitors and non-visitors. This lack of balance has been partially restored by David G. Erwin, in his pioneering investigation into what the Belfast public thought or knew about the Ulster Museum.[22] Erwin used the following simple questionnaire, with a statistically random sample of the Belfast population.

1 *Sex*   Male   Female

2 *Age*   0–12   13–19   20–29   30–39   40–49   50–59   60–69
70+

3 *Address (postal district)* 1 2 3 4 5 6 7 8 9 10 11 12 13 14 15

4 *Occupation*

5 *Have you ever been to the Ulster Museum?*
Yes   No
If answer to 5 No:

6 *Have you ever heard of the Ulster Museum?*
Yes   No

7 *How did you hear of it?*
Press/TV/Poster/A friend/Don't know/Other

8 *Where is it?* Armagh/Near Queen's Belfast/N'Ards Rd.
Belfast/Cultra/Don't know

9 *Why haven't you been?* Not interested/No way of getting there/Can never find the time/Others

10 *What would attract you to the Museum?*

The completed questionnaires revealed information which was either not available to Doughty or which differed markedly from his conclusions. Of the new information, the most significant was probably the ways in which people said they had heard about the Museum. Erwin found that 43 per cent knew of it 'from a friend', 37 per cent from television and 20 per cent from newspapers. The last two figures are surprising, because,

up to that time, the Museum had never mounted either a television or a newspaper campaign. Publicity had been acciden-
tal, in the form of news items, and Erwin concluded, very
reasonably, that the results of his survey suggested that money
spent on television would not be wasted.

The public divided itself according to this pattern:

Good attenders	Regular attenders	Bad attenders	Irregular attenders
Males Age 13–19 years	Males Age less than 19 years	Females	Females Age more than 39 years
People living close to the museum		People living far from the museum	
Skilled manual workers, clerical workers	Students, skilled workers. Unskilled and semi-skilled workers	Unskilled and semi-skilled workers. Housewives	Clerical workers, housewives, retired persons

In 1970 Herbert Coutts, of Dundee Museum, tried to assess
the attitude of visitors, not to the whole museum, but to one department, the Antiques Gallery, which he described, truthfully
but not very flatteringly, as 'a jumble of archaeology, local history and natural history'.[23] Somewhat to his surprise, 85 per
cent of the people questioned said they liked this kind of arrangement. 'It may be', he suggested, 'that many people were
content because they did not expect much of museum displays
in the first place. Also, a significant proportion of museum visitors may actually prefer to have palaeoliths displayed cheek-
by-jowl with butterflies. This gives the museum the air of a
mysterious treasure house with new discoveries to be made
round every corner – something which systematic display can
never do.'

An exceptionally interesting and imaginative survey was carried out in France during the mid-1960s by Pierre Bourdieu and
Alain Darbel.[24] Visitors to a number of art museums in Paris

and the provinces were sounded out by means of a questionnaire and their opinions presented partly in statistical form
and partly as quotations. Among other things, they were asked
this question: 'Which of these institutions reminds you most of
a museum: a church, a library, a court of law, a large store, a
court waiting room?' The replies varied a great deal, according
to whether the persons interviewed belonged to the working
class, middle class or upper class. 66 per cent of working class
people gave the answer 'a church', compared with 45 per cent of
the middle class and 30.5 per cent of the upper class. A museum
was felt to resemble a library by 9 per cent of the working class,
34 per cent of the middle class and 28 per cent of the upper class.
The other comparisons suggested as possibilities received
much less support.

The interviewees were also asked, 'In your opinion, what are
the best conditions for looking at a work of art? In particular, do
you yourself prefer to be with a lot of people or with very few
people?' The result was as follows:

	A lot of people	Few people	No preference	No answer
Working class	39	39	18	4
Middle class	11	67	15	11
Upper class	2	70	19.5	8.5

Working-class people said they felt happier to visit museums
and galleries in groups and liked to be provided with a guide,
even though the guide might talk above their heads. Educated
people, who were best equipped to understand what the guides
were saying, were the most anxious not to go round the museum with them.

Of the working-class visitors 55 per cent were unable to think
of the name of a single painter. Those who could produce a
name always picked painters, such as Leonardo, Michaelan-
gelo and Rembrandt, who were well back in history or those
who had, like Van Gogh and Renoir, been the subject of films,
or whose paintings had been widely reproduced. A Lille house-
wife said, 'I like pictures with Christ in them', a Lens shopkeeper admitted, 'I didn't understand Picasso', and a Lille
factory worker explained why, for him, it was important to
remain silent in a museum. 'You're frightened of meeting a con-

noisseur', he told the interviewer. 'Anyone like me comes and goes without speaking to anyone.'

These reactions may possibly have been more typical of France than of certain other countries, but everywhere the ignorance and prejudice of museum visitors has been very little studied, although there is plenty of evidence available to those with the patience to seek it out and piece it together. Civic worthies and church authorities, for example, have frequently turned their attention to statues and paintings of nude figures in local art galleries. A particularly ludicrous instance of this occurred in Buffalo, New York, in 1911, when the city's Board of Aldermen unanimously passed a resolution demanding that nude statues in the Albright Fine Arts Academy should be draped.

There was a heated controversy in the local press. The *Buffalo Times* had a leading article,[25] headed 'Who would have thought it?' The opening paragraph showed little inclination to take the aldermen very seriously. 'We find ourselves in danger', it began, 'of losing sight of the gravity of Alderman Sullivan's proposal regarding the statues in the Albright Gallery, in a sense of surprise that the Alderman from the First Ward takes such an interest in art. We wouldn't have suspected him of ever getting near enough to these figures to be shocked at them, and whether they shall be equipped with gowns and trousers or not, we are willing to wager that sculpture has a future in Buffalo, now that our city fathers are beginning to wake up to its demoralizing possibilities.'

The *Buffalo Courier* took the line that 'the matter of the resolution offered by one of the aldermen to require the draping of statuary in the Buffalo Art Gallery is chiefly suggestive of the permanent offense to public decency which the retention in office of certain members of the aldermanic board constitutes.'[26] There were some excellent headlines.

NUDE STATUES MUST BE
CLOTHED OR OSTRACIZED
SO DECLARE CITY FATHERS

But Directors of Albright Art Gallery Express No Alarm
Over Fate of High Art – Sentiment Exists Among

Art Experts That Aldermen Are Pursuing Fair
Creatures in Unfatherly Manner

DIRECTORS, HOWEVER, THROUGH
DEFERENCE WILL "INVESTIGATE"

BISHOP COLTON WOULD SEGREGATE NUDE
STATUES AT THE ALBRIGHT ART GALLERY

Eminent Catholic Prelate Believes They Have A
Blighting and Demoralizing Influence
on Many People

CLERGY AND PUBLIC AGREE

Belief is General that the Exhibition is Harmful, Especially to
Boys and Girls, and Should be Isolated

The question of when a nude was erotic, and therefore objectionable, and when it was artistically cold and safe, was not
solved, and the statues remained undraped. Some of them were
eventually given to the University of Buffalo, which, as an educational institution, was entitled to all the nudes it cared to
house.

Incidents such as this have occurred repeatedly throughout
the nineteenth and twentieth centuries in all countries. Public
bodies have a way of believing that museums and art galleries
should be safe places, containing nothing likely to offend the
most timid and conservative members of the public, and
nothing which might disturb the *status quo* in any way. The ideal
exhibit, so far as Buffalo was concerned, was Sir John Everett
Millais' painting, *Little Mrs. Gamp*, showing a child with a large
umbrella. This, the Buffalo *Evening News* declared, was 'the delight of the gallery visitors'[27] and 'her green umbrella is so
English that it is a veritable cockney in itself.' *Academy Notes*
went further. 'There are certain pictures', it said,[28] 'which
appeal at once to the popular taste – and this in no way is to be
considered as necessarily deprecatory of their artistic quality,
though it must be admitted that prose is more generally understood than poetry, and that the easily assimilated theme is more

popularly successful than the superlatively fine technical triumph.'

In the Socialist countries, the professed aim of the educational system is to raise the whole population to a high cultural level and to produce 'many-sided and harmoniously developed socialist personalities', and museums are naturally seen to have an important part to play in this. To sharpen their powers of observation and to encourage them to develop a personal response to works of art, schoolchildren in the German Democratic Republic are required to write down their impressions of selected works during their visits to art galleries. Two examples of the results of this process of self-interrogation will indicate the possibilities.

(a) On Bert Heller's portrait of the President, Wilhelm Pieck.

> I am standing in front of the portrait of Wilhelm Pieck. His friendly eyes look straight at me below his bushy eyebrows. The expression on his face shows not only kindliness but determination. It is like a silent command, not just to keep going forward, but to listen to what he has to say first. His face tells of a life of anxiety and deprivation. The high forehead, the hair combed smoothly back are characteristic of a reflective, studious man, eager for knowledge. One can see he was a man who was driven on to acquire new experiences during every day of his long life.[29]

(b) On Paul Michaelis' painting, *High-School Girl*.

> I don't know this girl personally, and yet she isn't a stranger to me. I understand what she's thinking. On many points, our opinions are the same. I would do many of the things she does. If I were to look for her, I should find her everywhere in our country. I could look for her in Berlin, Leipzig or Dresden and I could find her a hundred times over. She could be one of my classmates, she could be myself. She is a girl with her weak points and her strong points, but she knows what she's aiming at, and she's going to get there. She knows what life's about, for herself and for everyone else.

It is easy to say that neither of these two pictures was of any great merit and that the boys and girls who were brought to look at them had thoroughly conditioned minds before they came, so that the passages quoted above contain nothing but second-hand, approved thoughts. But suppose, instead of a seventeen-year-old German child in 1971, we had an English boy or girl faced with a picture of Lord Kitchener in 1914 or of Winston Churchill in 1942. Would the responses have been so very much more original, more unpredictable? In any period, and in any country, a truly personal reaction is a rare phenomenon. There are fashions of thought in the United States, just as much as in the Soviet Union; and any research, of whatever kind, which is carried on among museum visitors can do little more than tune in to the current fashion, which may be highly unpleasant to the museum staff, especially if they belong to a different generation or to a different cultural group.

The difficulty of which most curators of large museums are well aware is that they and the members of their professional staff are highly educated people and that many of their visitors are nothing of the kind. They naturally wish to improve this situation, to bring visitors closer to their own level of taste and knowledge; but they disagree, often fundamentally, as to how this can best be done and more than a few have come to believe that the attempt is futile, that the serious work of the museum should go on behind closed doors, while the public is given a circus to keep it amused and contented.

It may well be that those who are most successful in communicating with ordinary people are very close to being ordinary people themselves, and that, in the museum field as in others, the mandarin attitude, however well-intentioned, is doomed to failure. The present author has a collection of letters sent to him by people in charge of small museums in the United States. The letters are often hand-written, and not always entirely literate. They come from enthusiastic, devoted men and women with no museum training or career ambitions, people who do not move in the great world of research and publications at all.[30] They are the museum curators who rarely attend conferences and never complete questionnaires, and who prefer to describe their collections in a rambling and warm-hearted, rather than a scientific way.

'I have had the museum opened five years', writes one man, 'doors never locked, people come and go at their desires. I do not expect to lock the doors until someone takes something then I will keep it locked from 10 p.m. to 7 a.m.' His museum has

> more than 200 pieces of gourd craft from Ecuador South America, lots of crafts from peru as well as crafts and gourds as they are used as containers from all over the globe. Four different persons are making Indian Musical instruments and sending them to the Museum. We have two carved by Theo Schoon of New Zealand. He is considered the World's best carver.

The curator of a museum in Kentucky has a collection of great public interest, 'in one of the first banks robbed by the notorious Jesse James gang (1868)'. It shows, he tells us, 'the original bank vaults, dating from 1857, antique furnishings of mid-19th century and artifacts relating to early Kentucky history and to Jesse James'. The museum is open on a rather irregular basis, the best visiting time obviously being 'during local Tobacco Festival', since 'Jesse James' robbery is re-enacted at this time'.

At a museum in Texas the collection illustrates

> the Texana West, including items used in the household, general store, fire arms, old tools for construction, old time cobblers' tools, as well as old locks, keys, etc. In other words any thing that people needed to develope the Old West, I have in my Museum.

Museums of this type – and there are a great many of them scattered throughout the world – tend to have collections of a very general nature, often, if not usually, arranged in a way that makes a professionally trained curator despair, but which the public seems to like. They can be welded into the local community with a friendly solidity that the large museum may often yearn for but cannot achieve. A museum with a staff of experts is, inescapably, in a 'we-and-they' position with regard to the general public. During the past twenty-five years especially, many of the most creative people in the museum world have come to believe that such a position is sterile, in that it prevents a museum from helping those who could most benefit from help and encouragement. The neighbourhood or community museum, in which local people are closely and continuously involved from the beginning, sees no cultural or power gap between the people who plan and run the museum and the people who use it. One of the most remarkable and most successful of such museums, MUSE, in Brooklyn, New York, has rejected the conventional geographical definition of 'community' in favour of something wider. 'I like to think of it', says Lloyd Hezekiah, the man in charge, 'as something called the "community of interest" or the "community of concern", which cuts across any narrow geographical boundaries around any one institution. It cuts across social, economic, ethnic and all other kinds of interrelated barriers. It's like a spider's web reaching out wherever it can cling. That's how I define the word "community".'[30]

Mr Hezekiah has never carried out any surveys to find out what kind of people his museum attracts and where they come from, although he hopes to do this one day, on an informal basis – he is 'usually against official surveys or things of this sort'. Meanwhile, he has local musicians who come to play in the museum, consumer workshops, public-speaking groups, activities of all kinds. The idea of a museum as a cathedral or a temple is, he believes, completely out of date. 'My personal belief is', he says, 'that a museum is a theater.

> There are many parallels. I look at the theater building as being a museum building. I look at the content of a museum as the play that's running in the theater. I look at the design of the exhibits as being analogous to the props the actor uses on stage. But the actor has to use the proper props to bring life into the play. And similarly, the museum visitor, I think, is the actor, who has to interrelate with what is presented and exhibited to get the juices flowing and to get the production to come alive.[31]

So MUSE has its producers and designers on the stage with the actors. The staff are not locked away in their offices and laboratories all the time. They spend a large part of each working week moving round among the visitors – who, in this case, are largely children – finding out how they react to the displays, which experiments are successful, which are not. This is their form of research. It is not statistically reliable, but it works and it keeps the museum in touch with the public in a way that a questionnaire can never do. At MUSE, market research has become human, which is to say, professionally suspect.

But there is a strong tide flowing in that direction. Dr Peter H. Pott, the Director of the National Museum of Ethnology at Leiden, in the Netherlands, has pointed out[37] that most museums are still arranged in the patronising way that was normal in the nineteenth century. Visitors are treated like children, to be given a selection of information which wiser and more erudite people believe will be good for them. This, says Dr Pott, 'unconsciously creates an element of resistance in a rapidly evolving society, which since the beginning of this century has shown a continuously decreasing willingness to be led.' For this reason, he believes, museum directors can no longer be 'well-educated persons with good taste, who protect the things that are entrusted to their care'. The new breed will be

> conversationalists in the widest sense of the word, living in the present day of a continually changing world and continually changing circumstances. They must be able and prepared to receive any group of visitors on the basis of that group's interests and level of development. In short, they must be the perfect host, who enjoys and understands the things around him and whose greatest pleasure is to share with others the feelings of admiration and wonder which fill him and which give color to everyday life.

The most recent evidence suggests that, in Britain at least, there is a long way to go before Dr Pott's goal is reached. A survey carried out in November 1973 by a market research firm on behalf of the *Illustrated London News*[33] showed that, in the four large London museums investigated – the National Portrait Gallery, the Tate Gallery, the Natural History Museum and the Science Museum – 'visitors are overwhelmingly drawn from the middle classes . . . there is a consistent and depressing absence of working-class visitors.' The evidence points to regular visitors being 'a highly selective, élite band of people'. The percentage of visitors whose full-time education extended to 18 and beyond was roughly the same for all four museums, although the Tate Gallery appears to attract the largest share:

National Portrait Gallery	Tate Gallery	Natural History Museum	Science Museum
71	83	74	79

The distribution of visitors according to social class was:

	National Portrait Gallery	Tate Gallery	Natural History Museum	Science Museum
A	3	8	6	5
B	31	36	28	27
C¹	43	45	35	43
C²	17	8	17	11
D	4	2	9	8
E	0	0	3	3
not stated	1	0	3	3

One third of the population of Britain is reckoned to fall into classes D and E, but at the Tate Gallery only 2 per cent of the visitors come from these two classes, while the highest figure, at the Natural History Museum, is only 12 per cent. We do not, as yet, have comparable, up-to-date figures for other countries. It would be most useful to know if the situation is markedly different in, say, the Soviet Union or Norway, or if there, too, museum visitors are still mainly what Dr Pott calls, in something approaching despair, 'right-minded and respectable people'.

PLATES

1. AUSTRALIA

Museum of Applied Arts and Sciences, Sydney, N.S.W. Part of the collection, before 1910.

This bears a strong resemblance to an antique dealer's showroom. The label-cards might well be price-tickets. Items of a wide range of periods and styles are jumbled absurdly together, with no attempt to suggest how they looked in their original surroundings, as pieces of furniture to be used and lived with.

An arrangement of this kind presupposes a very small number of adult visitors. A steady rush of school parties would be disastrous and unhandlable.

Western Australian Museum, Perth, W.A. Interior, early 1900s.

A classic example of the old, boxed-in method of display. The bear and the lion appear to come off particularly badly, being placed in what are, in effect, glass-panelled carrying-cases or coffins. The only concession to life is to permit the animals to stand up. The kangaroos are shown a little more realistically but one is never able to forget the case and the surrounding exhibits.

This room is really a filing system. As such, its most successful feature is the brilliant top-lighting — there is no evidence of any artificial lighting. This type of lighting does absolutely nothing, however, to create an atmosphere for the creatures in the cases. No distinction is drawn between a rock and a tiger in this respect. One is looking at what are firmly conceived as scientific specimens.

The unfortunate turtles clapped against the wall at the far end are mere artefacts, pieces of sculpture of just the right size to fill up convenient blank spaces.

2. AUSTRIA

Kunsthistorisches Museum, Vienna. Interior of Room 32, 1972.

The Kunsthistorisches Museum is saddled with a building which no modern museum curator could possibly want or design. The room-by-room division imposes an unfortunate rigidity on the plan and induces a feeling of hopelessness in the visitor, who never knows how much more there is to see beyond the next door and the next door and the next door. To see 'Saal XXXII' above the doorway is to be reminded of a meeting with a very long agenda, which cannot possibly be finished in the time.

Even so, the Curator has done what he can to introduce variety, fluidity and, within the limitations placed on him, surprise and excitement. The spirit of the tapestry is echoed in the sculptures, each of which is provided with four little pillars which poke fun at the giant nineteenth-century pillar and prevent us from taking our ancestors too seriously. The placing of the sculptures, in a free arrangement round the room, emphasises the designer's intention to create a stage, rather than a fully-enclosed space. The effect is that of a theatre, rather than of a museum gallery. It is a most interesting example of the way in which appalling disadvantages can be successfully overcome.

Kunsthistorisches Museum, Vienna. Room 1, 1971.

Fifty years ago, this room contained twice the number of paintings that it does today. A determined attempt has been made to defeat the huge and palatial character of the room, partly by exploiting the space in order to give a feeling of peace and relaxation, and partly by using a broad white band to divide the room horizontally into two rooms, placed one above the other, a floor room and a ceiling room. The ceiling can be appreciated as a work of art in its own right, from the upholstered comfort of the sofas.

It is, incidentally, a stroke of genius to provide such luxurious seats in Room 1. In Room 20, perhaps, where exhaustion could reasonably be setting in, one might have perhaps expected them and been grateful for them, but to have them in Room 1 suggests that the visit can be undertaken at an easy pace and that, with luck, weariness need never set in at all.

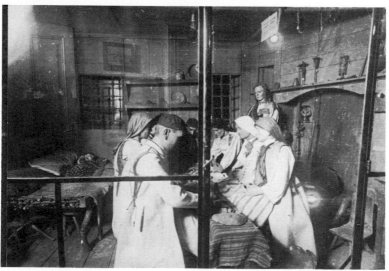

3. BULGARIA

National Ethnographical Museum and Institute, Sofia. Early displays.

This section of the museum, photographed in the early 1920s, reflects the growing national consciousness in Bulgaria at that time, and a wish to commemorate, if not preserve, the traditions and customs of the country. An attempt was made to show costumes, tools and household equipment in settings which bore as close a resemblance as possible to the conditions in which they had been actually used. There is, it will be noticed, a minimum of labelling. Each exhibit is left to tell its own story, which it does perfectly effectively. One sees these peasants and craftsmen among their possessions and one gets a feeling of the quality of their life. What exactly each separate item in the display may be is of quite secondary importance.

Nationalism can do strange things to museums. In deference to the strength and traditions of Slovak nationalism, some of the more important museums in Czechoslovakia have to be duplicated with, for example, two major museums devoted to science and technology, and two to art and ethnography. In one way, this may be no bad thing, since travel to the metropolis can be expensive, tiring and time-wasting, but, whether in Czechoslovakia or anywhere else, museums which see themselves primarily as prestige symbols are apt to dissipate their energies and their money unduly on large, expensive masses of masonry, and to regard the arrangement of the collections as something which can be financed only once. The displays at Martin illustrate this, although not in such an extreme form as, say, the Musée de l'Homme in Paris, where there has been no money even to replace the faded and yellowing labels of the mid-1930s. The cases shown in the pictures contain superb examples of traditional Slovak clothing, embroidery and lace, but, by modern standards, the style of display is hopelessly congested and out of date. Nationalism dictates that Martin has wonderful things, but it does not, unfortunately, provide the funds needed to make the most of them.

4. CANADA

Main Street, Barkerville, British Columbia, looking south.

This nineteenth-century mining town has been preserved, more or less complete, as Barkerville Historic Park. It is an open-air museum, where it all happened. The signposting and advertising is mostly discreet, and the buildings and their contents have been left to speak for themselves. There are no vehicles, no horses, no people dressed in pioneer clothes. The town is unashamedly dead and it is as an embalmed corpse that it offers itself, very successfully, to the people who drive in to see it.

The United States, especially in the western areas, is generously supplied with what one might call village-street or town-street museums. These are of two types – a genuine street, as at Alamo Village, Bracketville, Texas, restored and preserved for the benefit of posterity, and, as at the Desert Caballeros Western Museum, Wickenburg, Arizona, a replica of old-time buildings, showing their scale and variety. One of the problems of the genuine buildings is that they are usually made of wood, and need a great deal of maintenance. The replicas are, of course, brand-new – too much so for some tastes – and, if they are put inside a museum building, well safeguarded against the destructive effects of time and weather.

The buildings are by no means everything. They offer a convenient opportunity to demonstrate old customs, furniture, guns and pioneer equipment, and also to sell souvenirs more or less reminiscent of the past. These may range from biscuits to jewellery, and from replicas of six-shooters to small bags of pieces of rock. The nostalgia for pioneer days is very powerful in both the United States and Canada, and citizens of both countries are willing to drive long distances in order to establish emotional links with the past in this way.

5. CHINA, PEOPLE'S REPUBLIC

Entrance to Spirit Tablet Hall of Confucian Temple, Ch'iifu, Shantung Province.

In today's China, Confucianism and the former Imperial Family are as safely obsolete and of the past as the Orthodox Church and the Romanovs are in the Soviet Union. China finds no philosophical or political problem in preserving the old temples and palaces as museums, which can do visitors no harm and which, as exhibitions of splendid craftsmanship, serve to emphasise the achievements of past generations.

China is not rich in museums of the Western type, repositories where valuable objects are brought together so that visitors can see them with ease, but away from their original context and significance. The typical Chinese museum is a building of historic or aesthetic importance, preserved as nearly as possible in its original condition and with its original furnishings.

At a first glance, a number of Chinese museums — that at Loyang, in Honan Province, is a good example — appear to bear a close resemblance to those which are traditional in the West, in that material has been brought to a special building in order to be shown to the public; but there are two important differences. The first is philosophical — the museum is meant to increase the cultural and political awareness of the visitors, that is, to leave them better citizens than it found them, and the second organisational — no division is made between exhibits from the past and exhibits of the present. A museum, in the Chinese sense, may quite properly contain both tractors and jade carvings. It exists to raise the level of public knowledge, and since the fully instructed man and woman is adequately informed about both tractors and jade, it is a matter of convenience to display both under the same roof.

Village of Yeh S'ing, near Juichin, Kiangsi Province. As the site of an early guerilla base of the Revolutionary Army, the entire village has been preserved. The house shown in the picture is the one lived in by Mao Tse-tung.

This photograph illustrates the extent to which the stock of site-museums is being constantly enlarged in China. The nation's museums are required to keep up with history. Museums of the historic-house type are very likely to be in remote areas and, under Chinese conditions, accessible only by special buses. This means that visitors will nearly always arrive in groups, and that they will respond to the museum as a group. The museum consequently functions as a constant encouragement to national solidarity.

6. CYPRUS

Cyprus Folk Art Museum, Nicosia.

This excellent little museum, in a wing of the old Archbishop's Palace, has been created during the past twenty-five years by an enthusiastic schoolmaster, with a very small government grant to support his efforts. The material in it — tools, handicrafts and folk art — has been gathered together at the last possible moment, before Cyprus became fashionable and wealthy private collectors moved in to mop up the contents of cottages and farms. The museum possesses great charm and, apart from an expert curator, practically no staff. The building and its contents are in perfect harmony and, of great importance in the Cyprus heat, the old style of construction, with thick stone walls, keeps the rooms cool even in summer. The atmosphere is peaceful and unhurried.

The contrast with the prestigious Cyprus Museum, also in Nicosia, is very marked. The Cyprus Museum is dedicated to the archaeology of Cyprus. It is an entirely professional establishment, with the full panoply of departmental keepers, technicians, library and scholarly publications. The splendid collections, entirely of objects discovered in the island, are displayed in a chaste and restrained fashion, the total effect being that of a mini-British museum, where the visitor is left in no doubt that what the museum regards as its serious work goes on behind the scenes and that he is privileged to see what is no more than the tip of the iceberg.

7. CZECHOSLOVAKIA

National Technical Museum, Prague. Display in the Department of Photography.
Model of atmospheric mine-pumping engine, early eighteenth century.

The National Technical Museum has one of the finest photographic sections in the world, covering both still and moving picture photography. Great pains have been taken to weld the mass of exhibits into a coherent story and to avoid overwhelming the visitor with details which are too technical for him to absorb. It is a presentation which makes the photographers as important as their equipment. On the whole, however, the effect is rather static. The material stays safely and quietly in its cases and, although sporadic use is made of films and slides, for most of the day and on most days, nothing much happens. The contrast with the newly arranged Department of Photography at the Smithsonian in Washington is very marked. Here, a huge budget has been devoted to bringing the collections to life wherever possible. Today's photographic techniques have been used to illustrate and explain yesterday's photographic techniques.

The National Technical Museum is absurdly cramped for space. It has not yet been able to recover all the buildings allocated to it before the 1939–45 war. A large part of the collections has to be kept more or less permanently in the kind of storage which does not encourage research and, although temporary exhibitions are arranged as often as funds permit, the Technical Museum is never allowed to forget that it is, compared with the National Museum, which looks after art and history, a poor relation. The paradox is a curious one in a country where industrial and technical progress is a much publicised article of faith.

8. DENMARK

Museum at the Royal Arsenal, Copenhagen.

The Danes sometimes have a curious sense of what is appropriate
— the National War Museum is in a former church — but the
Arsenal Museum is in every way right. The combination of the
building and its contents helps the visitor to build up a better understanding of both war and monarchy in the days of wooden battle-
ships. This museum suggests, rather than explains, the elegance
and toy-sailor qualities of the old-style warfare, without losing sight
of its crudity and brutality. Where it fails is where most military and
naval museums fail, in pointing out the huge proportion of the
national budget, wrung from a people that was far from wealthy,
that went towards satisfying the prestige and ambitions of national
rulers. Anyone who enters such a museum should begin by asking,
'What is missing here?'

9. EGYPT

Egyptian Museum, Cairo. Dwarf engraved on lid of sarcophagus.

The Egyptian Museum is, as it should be, the permanent home of many of the finest items to be discovered in the course of nineteenth- and twentieth-century excavations. It is therefore a sad irony that the Tutankhamen treasures should have been so much better shown during their temporary sojourn at the British Museum than in the Museum at Cairo where they belong. The Egyptian Museum is, to put the matter brutally, shabby and old-fashioned. The reason is not far to seek: it has not yet recovered from the departure of the British, under whose influence and during whose presence it was born. A highly nationalistic but very poor new state, obsessed with the need to create huge military forces, has had little money or energy to spare for the modernisation of museums. When the new tourist trade begins this will no doubt be put right, but meanwhile such beautiful items as the one illustrated will have little opportunity to do themselves justice. They are waiting, one hopes patiently, for a style of architecture and display appropriate to the 1980s and to Egypt's new place in the world.

10. FINLAND

Archaeological Department of the State Historical Museum (now National Museum of Finland), Helsinki, as it was in 1906.

An excellent example of the reference type of arrangement, planned primarily for the use of scholars, but accessible at certain times to well-behaved members of the public. The table and chairs emphasise the working atmosphere of the room.

11. FRANCE

Musée d'Unterlinden, Colmar, Alsace. Replica of Alsatian wine cellar.

An atmosphere museum, in which genuine objects connected with the production of wine have been arranged in a room built to resemble a wine cellar in the smallest details. The only thing missing is the smell of wine, which is not at all difficult to produce, but which those in charge of such museums prefer, for some reason, to leave to the imagination of the visitors.

12. GERMAN FEDERAL REPUBLIC

Department of Metalworking, Deutsches Museum, Munich. Masterpieces of casting and forging, at a special exhibition, 1945.
Transport Museum, Nürnberg. Room devoted, among other things, to the Nürnberg-Fürth railway.

The Transport Museum at Nürnberg — the national museum — contains a number of original railway items, such as the locomotive shown in the picture. There is no lack of support, either in Germany or in other countries, for static railway museums of this type, and it would indeed be foolish to attempt to run venerable engines under steam. One has to remember, however, that a great many people in the world today are too young to have seen a steam locomotive working and that, faced with a museum specimen, they have to use a considerable amount of imagination to reconstruct the sounds and the feeling of a journey by steam-hauled train. Their fathers had no such problem, a locomotive in a museum immediately suggested a locomotive working on the track. This gap has to be filled by the museum in some way, by tapes, or by the occasional ride on a steam train, a refresher course, so to speak, which becomes more necessary with each generation that passes.

Elsewhere in the museum, there is a large collection of models illustrating the development of locomotives in Bavaria. This is essentially a reference library of locomotives and, as such, admirable for its purpose. It is, however, an expensive way of illustrating a catalogue, although the locomotives do, it is true, teach us at least as much about the art of model-building as about the history of steam engines in Bavaria.

13. GREAT BRITAIN

Dining Room, Saltram House, Plymouth, Devon. (*By permission of Tom Molland Ltd*)

Britain has, for its size, an incomparable number of great houses open to the public. The more popular they become with visitors, the more worrying the problem of wear and tear becomes. Carpets which were perfectly capable of withstanding a century of ordinary domestic use can look very different after only one season of well-publicised tourism, walls become grubby, precious objects get knocked down and broken, however well-guided the visitors may be. Yet, unless damage becomes catastrophic, which is rarely the case, the risk is worth running. A room such as this one at Saltram is an unequalled reminder of the effect that could be produced when craftsmen's wages were low and when wealth was concentrated in a very few hands.

14. NETHERLANDS

Windmills at Kinderdijk.

The seventeen windmills at Kinderdijk are of different types and date from the eighteenth and early nineteenth centuries. They were built to form an integrated pumping unit, for drainage purposes, and, although they have long since been replaced by electric pumps so far as work is concerned, they are kept in good condition, as a landscape feature which tourists in particular like to see, and as a set of technological monuments. The group of mills, sited where they have always been, is in the French term an eco-museum, a museum comprising an area and everything in it.

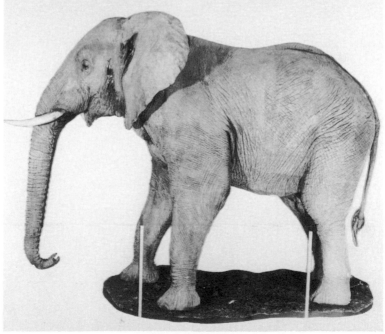

15. SOUTH AFRICA

South African Museum, Capetown. Bushman diorama.

This professionally excellent display, one of several in the Museum, uses glass-fibre figures and achieves a high degree of realism. The imagination and expertise which have gone to its creation are in themselves, however, a source of criticism and racial antagonism, since they have been devoted to showing the primitive way of life of non-white people in South Africa. To a coloured person, there is no essential difference between presenting a butterfly and a bushman to the world in this fashion. Both are the white man's specimens, symbols of his power and freedom to collect what pleases him. There are, in South African museums, no dioramas which illustrate the life and habits of white men and women. To present the master-race in this way would be politically explosive.

National Museum, Bloemfontein. Nearly completed fibre-glass replica of twenty-five year old bull elephant.

In the less sensitive field of animals and birds, South African museums have carried out superb display-work. The whole of this elephant, including the tusks (but not the eyes, which are glass), is made of glass-fibre. During the manufacturing process, the original body hairs of the animal have been incorporated in the casting material. The specimen weighs 700 pounds and is reckoned to be proof against the decay which attacks the work of even the most skilled taxidermist. Whether a replica of this kind can have the same emotional effect on visitors as the actual preserved corpse of a much-loved zoo animal is difficult to say.

At Oudtshoorn, Southern Cape, in the C. P. Nel Museum, there is an excellent exhibit devoted to the ostrich, showing the bird's life cycle and habitat. The fact that the ostrich has been around in Africa for a long time is emphasised by two rock engravings, 3000 years old, from the Sahara. This is a happy example of the effectiveness of breaking down the traditional barriers between museum 'subjects', in this case between zoology, archaeology and art.

With natural history, the imagination of the South African museum curator is unfettered. With people, it has to remain strictly within the political conventions.

16. SPAIN

Archaeological Museum, Seville. Hall of the Carambolo Treasure and Hall of Mercury.

These two displays use space in a prodigal way. They represent a complete swing away from the traditional museum method, in which each room contained as many objects as could be crammed into it, on the basis of the more the better. The sculptures and the gold ornaments are treated entirely as works of art, with no attempt whatever to present them as items in a series or a category. The visitor sees them as they are, without the distraction or support of background information or other exhibits. He is alone with them and has to rely on his own judgement and his own emotions.

17. SWEDEN

The Large Gallery in the Royal Museum, by Per Hilleström, 1796.

This painting, which shows part of the sculpture section at the Museum, is concerned mainly with Greek and Roman works. The busts, strung out like beads, present a somewhat ludicrous appearance – it is unwise to allow such easy comparisons to be made between one item and another, especially if they are of very unequal size and beauty – but the gallery as a whole forms a convenient promehade for elegant strolling and for meeting one's friends. It is, for the right people, a pleasant place to be, and the sculpture is of no great importance one way or another.

National Museum, Stockholm, 1886. The Grand Staircase and Entrance Hall in the year the Museum was opened. Engraved from a drawing by O. A. Mankell and G. Janet.

The Grand Staircase is grand in size, but not in materials or design. It follows the normal Victorian principle of taking visitors upwards to begin their tour of the Museum, in order to induce a suitably elevated state of mind; and one can see from their clothes that everyone in the picture is of superior social status.

One of the most magnificent and, by modern standards, absurd of Victorian entrance halls is still to be seen at the Fitzwilliam Museum, Cambridge (1848). The exhibition galleries were ornamented in the style of a palatial residence, with marble floors, columns of scagliola and elaborately plastered ceilings. Few museums had the money to reach the level of the Fitzwilliam, but throughout the nineteenth century it remained the ideal. The grandeur of the staircase was felt to be of much greater importance than its exhausting inconvenience to visitors.

18. SWITZERLAND

Kunsthaus, Zürich. Part of one of the galleries, before 1918.

The introduction of secure methods of hanging pictures without long cords or chains suspended from a rail, transformed the appearance of gallery walls. Previously, it was possible to conceal the cords only by totally covering each wall with pictures, and great ingenuity was often shown in producing this jigsaw puzzle effect. This photograph shows a not very acceptable compromise. The eye is given a chance to rest as it passes from item to item, and theoretically this should make it easier to concentrate on particular pictures. In practice, however, the chains steal the show as surely and completely as brassière straps seen through a transparent blouse. Hard as one may try to forget them, they are always there as a blemish on the presentation. But, the chains apart, the arrangement in the gallery necessitates a great deal of neck-craning, which is never a satisfactory position in which to attempt to appreciate a work of art.

Swiss Transport Museum, Luzern. Part of the section dealing with road transport.

The buildings are modern, simple and free from pomposity. They can be easily demolished, modified or added to, with no worries about vandalising a national monument. There are no enormous staircases up which the unfortunate visitor has to toil, no miles of corridors and acres of entrance halls to light, heat and clean. This is a cheaper place to run and the buildings perform admirably their function of sheltering the exhibits and of providing a flexible shell within which displays can be arranged and changed around with a minimum of difficulty. Here, in the room given up to horse-drawn carriages, the visitor is faced, immediately he comes down the short flight of steps, with a panel of skeleton carriages. The message is 'carriages came in many types and their shape and design is interesting and beautiful'. A single carriage, placed in front of the panel, links abstractions with reality, and there is then a natural transition to the carriages themselves. The lighting is adequate to allow everything to be clearly seen, but not so blatant and shop-like as to remove the strangeness and nostalgia which should always be present in a collection of objects which once formed part of everyday life, but which are now as dead as the people who used them.

19. UNITED STATES

Greenfield Village, Dearborn, Michigan. Nineteenth-century sternwheel steamer, 'Suwanee', cruising on miniature lagoon.

Ford money has been lavished on Greenfield Village, to make it an open-air museum which would outstrip all other open-air museums. The 'Suwanee' and the waterway provided for it is one small example of the Greenfield approach. This, Henry Ford believed, was how history should be absorbed, by coming face to face with the buildings and the objects that had formed part of the life of the past, all moved to a central site, so that historical awareness, like automobiles, could be produced efficiently and with a minimum of human effort. To bring the 'Suwanee' or Thomas Edison's laboratory to Dearborn might seem, to lesser mortals, a highly expensive and even wasteful business, but to Ford it was a normal type of industrial investment. One divided the price of the new equipment, the 'Suwanee' or Edison's laboratory, by the number of visitors it would produce, and any businessman could see that the cost per head was absurdly small, especially since each visitor would be seeing many items on the same day. Greenfield Village could well be the most heavily capitalised museum in the world.

**Merrimack Valley Textile Museum, North Andover, Massachu-
setts. Museum entrance lobby, with pattern of gear wheels.**

Merrimack was set up after the Second World War with industrial
money, in this case textile money. The family business concerned
was represented by a generation which was, by American standards, exceptionally cultured and public-spirited, and which felt an
urge to establish a museum which would do full justice to the industry which had enabled the family to live so comfortably for so
long. The result is a collection, a library and a centre of research
unequalled anywhere else in the world. The great machinery hall
contains all the items needed to document the development of textile manufacturing in America, arranged with a generosity of space
which makes study a pleasure instead of its normal purgatory, and,
in what might be termed the introductory departments, the visitor
is shown all he needs to know about materials, processes and products, with graphics, models, samples and original machines and
tools to communicate information and keep interest alive. Merrimack achieves a success which is very rare, a public show which
does not make the scholar uneasy.

APPENDIX I
Published reports of surveys of museum visitors

1897 Fechner, G. T., *Vorschule der Aesthetik*, Leipzig

1928 Robinson, Edward S., *The Behaviour of the Museum Visitor*, American Association of Museums

1929 Bloomburg, M., *An Experiment in Museum Instruction*, American Association of Museums

1930 'Pennsylvania Museum Classifies Its Visitors', *Museum News*, vol. 7 no. 15 (1 Feb)
Rea, Paul Marshall, 'How Many Visitors Should Museums Have?', *Museum News*, vol. 8 no. 1 (1 May)
Robinson, E. S., 'Psychological Problems of the Science Museum', *Museum News*, vol. 8 no. 5

1931 Robinson, E. S., 'Psychological Studies of the Public Museum', *School and Society*, no. 33 p. 839

1933 Melton, A. W., 'Some Behavioral Characteristics of Museum Visitors', *Psychological Bulletin*, no. 30

1934 Powell, Louis H., 'Evaluating Public Interest in Museum Rooms', *Museum News*, vol. 11 no. 15

1936 Melton, A. W.,'Distribution of Attention in Galleries in a Museum of Science and Industry', *Museum News*, vol. 14 no. 3
Melton, A. W., Feldman, Goldberg, Nita, and Mason, C. W., *Experimental Studies of the Education of Children in a Museum of Science*, American Association of Museums

1938 Porter, M. C., *Behaviour of the Average Visitor in the Peabody Museum of Natural History, Yale University*, American Association of Museums
Powell, Louis H., 'A Study of Seasonal Attendance at a Midwestern Museum of Science', *Museum News*, vol. 16 no. 3 (1 June)

1939 Coleman, Laurence Vail, 'Public Relations: Attendance', in *The Museum in America: A Critical Study*, vol. 2, American Association of Museums.

1940 Kearns, William E., 'Studies of Visitor Behavior at the Peabody Museum of Natural History, Yale University', *Museum News*, vol. 17 no. 14 (15 Jan)

1942 Yoshioka, Joseph G., 'A Direction-orientation Study with Visitors at the New York World's Fair', *Journal of Psychology*, vol. 27

1943 Calvei, Homer N., Derryberry, Mayhew, and Mensh, Ivan N., 'Use of Ratings in the Evaluation of Exhibits', *American Journal of Public Health*, vol. 33

1946 Nielson, L. C., 'A Technique for Studying the Behavior of Museum Visitors', *Journal of Educational Psychology*, vol. 37

1949 *Rapport betreffende jengdronleidingen in de musea voor beeldende kunsten* (Report on guided tours for young people in museums of fine art), Stedelijk Museum, Amsterdam

1952 Monzon, A., 'Bases para Incrementar el Publico que Visita el Museo Nacional de Antropologia' (A basis for increasing the number of visitors to the National Museum of Anthropology), *Anales del Instituto Nacional de Antropologia e Historia* (Mexico) vol. 6 part 2 no. 35

1953 Niehoff, Arthur, 'Characteristics of the Audience Reaction in the Milwaukee Public Museum', *Midwest Museums Quarterly*, vol. 13 no. 1
Sporer, W., 'Presentation of Exhibit Techniques and Methods to determine their Effectiveness', *Midwest Museums Quarterly*, vol. 13 no. 1

1955 Ewers, John, 'Problems and Procedures in Modernizing Ethnological Exhibits', *American Anthropologist*, vol. 57 no. 1

1956 Bigman, Stanley K., 'Art Exhibit Audiences', *Museologist* (Rochester) nos 59 and 60
Brooks, J. A., and Vernon, P. E., 'A Study of Children's Interests and Comprehension at a Science Museum', *British Journal of Psychology*, vol. 47 no. 3 (Aug)
Bureau of Social Science Research, Inc., Washington, *The Japanese House: a Study of Its Visitors and Their Reactions*
Niehoff, Arthur, 'The Physical Needs of the Visitor', *Lore* (Milwaukee Public Museum Quarterly) vol. 6 no. 4

Van der Hoek, G. J., 'Bezoekers Bekeken' (Characteristics of visitors), *Mededilingen Gemeentemuseum van den Haag* (The Hague) vol. 2 no. 2

1957 Bureau of Social Science Research, Inc., Washington, 'The Japanese Art Exhibit: A Study of Its Impact in Three Cities', *Clearing House for Western Museums Newsletter*, no. 211 (Sep)

1957 Goins, Alvin, and Griffenhagen, George, 'Psychological Studies of Museum Visitors and Exhibits at the U.S. National Museum', *Museologist*, no. 64
Reimann, Irving G., 'Post-Mortem on a Museum Questionnaire', *Museologist*, no. 63 (June)

1958 Goins, A. E., and Griffenhagen, George, 'The Effect of Location, and a Combination of Color, Lighting, and Artistic Design on Exhibit Appeal', *Museologist*, no. 67
Niehoff, Arthur, 'Evening Exhibit Hours for Museums', *Museologist*, no. 69 (Dec)
Reekie, Gordon, 'Toward Well-being for Museum Visitors', *Curator*, vol. 1 no. 1
Wright, G., 'Some Criteria for Evaluating Displays in Museums of Science and Industry', *Midwest Museums Quarterly*, vol. 18 no. 3

1959 Abbey, D. S., and Cameron, Duncan F., *The Museum Visitor: 1 – Survey Design*, Royal Ontario Museum
Niehoff, Arthur, 'Audience Reaction in the Milwaukee Public Museum: the Winter Visitors', *Midwest Museums Quarterly*, vol. 19 no. 2

1960 Abbey, D. S., and Cameron, Duncan F., *The Museum Visitor: 2 – Survey Results*, Royal Ontario Museum
Cameron, Duncan F., and Abbey, D. S., 'Investigating a Museum Audience', *Museologist*, no. 77 (Dec)
'Visits versus Visitors: an Analysis', surveys carried out at the Royal Ontario Museum, Toronto, *Museum News*, vol. 39 no. 3 (Nov)

1961 Abbey, D. S., and Cameron, Duncan F., *The Museum Visitor: 3 – Supplementary Studies*, Royal Ontario Museum
Abbey, D. S., and Cameron, Duncan F., 'Notes on Audience Research at the Royal Ontario Museum', *Museologist*, no. 80

1962 Cameron, Duncan F., and Abbey, D. S., 'Museum Audience Research: The Effect of an Admission Fee', *Museum News*, vol. 41 no. 3

Lotter, V., and Botha, E., 'Preliminary Survey of the Visiting Population of the South African Museum, Cape Town', *South African Museums Association Bulletin* (SAMAB) vol. 7 no. 14

Reese, David, and Moore, Emma, 'The Art Museum and the Public School: an Experiment', *Museum News*, vol. 40 no. 6

1963 Vowles, Valerie, 'The Uganda Museum, Kampala: The Public' *Museum*, vol. 16 no. 3

Weiner, George, 'Why Johnny Can't Read Labels', *Curator*, vol. 7 no. 2

1964 McDonald, Patricia M., *An Evaluation of the Educational Effectiveness of the Australian Museum Galleries*, The Australian Museum, Sydney, N.S.W.

Royal Ontario Museum, Toronto, *Three Reports on Visitor Surveys*

Smits, Edward J., 'A Suburban Museum Looks at its Visitors', *Museum News*, vol. 42 no. 9 (May), a survey carried out at the Nassau County Historical Museum, Long Island.

1965 Bourdieu, Pierre, and Darbel, Alain, *L'Amour de l'Art: les Musées et leur Public*, Paris

Christensen, Erwin V., 'Labels for Masterpieces', *Museum News*, vol. 43 no. 9 (May)

Parsons, Lee A.,'Systematic Testing of Display Techniques for an Anthropological Exhibit', *Curator*, vol. 8 no. 2

Parsons, Lee A., and Borhegyi, Stephan F. de, 'The Milwaukee Public Museum: Display of Collection', *Museum*, vol. 17 no. 1

Waters, Somerset R., 'Museums and Tourism', *Museum News*, vol. 44 no. 4 (Dec)

1968 Doughty, P S., 'The Public of the Ulster Museum: a statistical survey', *Museums Journal*, June and Sep, pp. 19–25, 47–53

Shettel, Harris H., 'An Evaluation of Existing Criteria for Judging the Quality of Science Exhibitions', *Curator*, vol. 11 no. 2

1969 Johnson, D. A., 'Museum Attendance in the New York Metropolitan Region', *Curator*, vol. 12 no. 3

Musement gemeten (A museum assessment): an opinion survey of visitors to museums in the Netherlands, carried out on behalf of the Ministry of Culture, Recreation and Social Work, Stedelijk Museum, Amsterdam

Rapport van een onderzoek onder de bezoekers van het Stedelijk Museum (Report of an enquiry carried out among visitors to the Stedelijk Museum), Stedelijk Museum, Amsterdam

1970 Owen, David E., 'Are national museums in the provinces necessary?' (a brief survey of Manchester visitors to London museums), *Museums Journal*, vol. 70 no. 1 (June)

1971 Coutts, Herbert, 'The Antiquities Gallery of Dundee Museum: a visitor survey', *Museums Journal*, vol. 70 no. 4 (Mar)

Erwin, David G., 'The Belfast Public and the Ulster Museum: a statistical survey', *Museums Journal*, vol. 70 no. 4 (Mar)

1973 'Visitors to the City of Norwich Museums, 1971–72', *Museums Journal*, vol. 72 no. 4 (Mar)

1974 Mason, Tim, 'The visitors to Manchester Museum: a questionnaire survey', *Museums Journal*, vol. 73 no. 4 (Mar)

Barton, Kenneth, 'Recording attendances at Portsmouth City Museums: the method and its effect', *Museums Journal*, vol. 73 no. 4 (Mar)

APPENDIX II

Questionnaire used by Milwaukee Public Museum in 1964, in connexion with an anthropological exhibit

I GENERAL INFORMATION

1 Did you know you were going to be 'tested' before you looked at the exhibit? Yes ( ); No ( )

2 Did you fill out a questionnaire on the Environment and Culture exhibit (or other exhibit in this case) previously? Yes ( ), No ( )

3 The main reason you stopped to look at this exhibit is . . . . (Check One) the pretty pictures ( ); the interesting Indian crafts ( ); the attractive design ( ); I was curious about the topic ( ); the familiar objects from our own culture ( ); other people were looking at it ( ); I was asked to ( ); I look at everything ( ); another reason? ————

4 You are: Male ( ); Female ( )

5 Your age group is: under 13 years ( ); 13–17 ( ); 18–24 ( ); 25–39 ( ); 40–65 ( ); over 65 years ( )

6 Highest year of school completed. Circle correct year.
1 2 3 4 5 6 7 8   9 10 11 12   13 14 15 16   Over
Elementary   High   College   Grad. School
School   School

7 Have you had any anthropology courses? Yes ( ); No ( )

8 What kind of work do you do?————————————————

9 Where do you live?

    City ———————— County ———————— State ————————

II IN YOUR OPINION . . .

1 The exhibit topic is presented in a manner that is . . . understandable (   ); understandable, but complicated (   ); confused (   )

2 Did you learn something new from the exhibit?   Yes (   );
No (   )

3 I enjoyed the exhibit . . . very much (   ); average (   ); not at all (   )

4 The exhibit labels are . . . too detailed (   ); not detailed enough (   ); just about right (   )

5 I found the exhibit . . . colors satisfactory (   ); too colorful (   ); too plain (   )

6 The number of utensils shown is . . . too many (   ); too few (   ); just about right (   )

7 The number of Indian areas shown is . . . too many (   ); too few (   ); just about right (   )

8 Other criticism . . . —————————————————————

III QUIZ

1 Geographical surroundings affec-   True (   )
ted the ways in which different   False (   )
Indians lived.   Exhibit doesn't tell (   )

2 The materials Indians selected for   True (   )
their crafts strongly reflect the   False (   )
environment in which they lived.   Exhibit doesn't tell (   )

3 Most North American Indians,   True (   )
in spite of great differences in   False (   )
environment, made some kind of   Exhibit doesn't tell (   )
spoons and water containers.

4 More advanced cultures, such as   True (   )
our own, depend less directly upon   False (   )

their environment than more primitive cultures, such as the Plains Indians.

Exhibit doesn't tell ( )

5 The main reason that Plains Indians did not make utensils out of mountain sheep horn is . . .

(a) horn was hard to carve with primitive tools ...... ( )
(b) buffalo horn was closer at hand than mountain sheep horn .... ( )
(c) mountain sheep horn is not as smooth as buffalo horn .... ( )
(d) mountain sheep were difficult to hunt or capture .... ( )

THANK YOU FOR YOUR COOPERATION

APPENDIX III
A selection of comments made by members of the public at the Museum of Non-Objective Painting, New York

The report is prefaced by this note: '*The visitors' names and addresses, together with their unsolicited comments, are on record in the Museum of Non-Objective Painting, owned by the Solomon R. Guggenheim Foundation, 1071 Fifth Avenue, New York City. They give evidence that never before has there been art, equally effective, equally uplifting, and equally practical.*'

If man today should find himself restless and without inspiration, the answer would come to him that he is too materialistically minded, too absorbed in matter. He would realise that his soul is starved and longing for spiritual nourishment. One only has to see this collection, which is far more beautiful than any material possession could ever be. From these paintings come forth a shining light, a warmth of spiritual tenderness embracing one's very being. No other art form has ever given so strong a conviction of making one realize how devastating material treasures can become where there is no vision.

Had it not been for the taxi strike, I would never have been on patrol in this district, and therefore might have gone on for a long time in ignorance of the existence of this museum. You may find it incongruous to think of the police having interests in the fine arts, but as a matter of fact, there are more painters and musicians in our precinct than anything else. Many of us who have to make a living wish to paint or compose, but are doing patrol work for the time being. Actually, I am a musician, and for a long time it has worried me to think that I can't reconcile all that I feel through music, and all that which I try and express in my own compositions, with any other medium. I know a terribly strong spiritual power which exists within my soul when I listen to music, but now for the first time painting has awakened a response from my inner understanding of a sphere beyond reality.

Your new exhibition is magnificent. In scope, in breadth, in originality, and in technical mastery, it far surpasses any exhibition we've had in New York for years, and I follow them all! Of course it's the painting itself that makes this such a landmark in the history of modern art; but the perfect taste and judgment shown in the framing and hanging does its part. What luck to have a creative artist as a director! No wonder this is the most beautiful museum in the country.

When I was in a veterans' hospital outside Los Angeles, a fellow there had some reproductions of non-objective painting. We used to kid him a lot about them, but gradually they began to 'come through' to us, just as he said. They kind of get under your skin, and you don't realise how much they are affecting you. I began to want to be neater, and not only get my things in order but get my whole life organized. It was like starting all over again with a clean slate. I'm very grateful to the people whose courage and foresight made it possible for my life to become enriched by non-objective painting.

I was a very nervous child. When I grew up I went to many different psychiatrists, until I had reached the point of speechlessness. Now I am curing myself in my own way – by a sense of creation and beauty. These paintings have a wonderful restfulness, and a joy of creative imagination which nothing else I have done or seen can approach. I am particularly in tune with the wonderful Rebay water-colours on the second floor. They sweep the cobwebs from my tired mind.

This museum is a haven of restfulness and tranquility, yet the air is vibrant with living zest and vitality. I feel I owe a great debt to the painters represented here, and to those responsible for the organization, for my afternoon here has done far more for me than any doctor or psychologist could do. For weeks I have been feeling nervous, worried and altogether ill. It was as though life itself was too much for me and no amount of self-analysis could bring my thoughts into line. But in these paintings I seem to see a rational, logical pattern which somehow is a visual interpretation of how my own personal activities should be organised. It has given me confidence and determination, and I shall go home with these reproductions of these lovely paintings that have been my salvation.

The last time I visited your museum, there was a group of school children being shown around. I was fascinated by their reactions to the paintings. Their approach was so natural and instinctive. They first explained about the colours, and the flow of lines, and the variety of shapes. Their responses were keenly felt, and their observations were sincere and intelligent. This may sound funny, but my appreciation was increased tremendously by the spontaneity of the children.

As an electrical engineer, non-objective painting is the only kind of painting that has any meaning for me. I can appreciate the necessities of space and form and color composition envisioned and made visible in each painting in the museum collection, so that each is an achievement of inspired and developed harmony. It is as if each painting were the presentation, through truth, of the imagery of the spirit.

This museum has really been my salvation, in a way, for the type of work I have to do for a living had put me in a bad rut. My work really depends on draftsmanship and offers little scope for creative work. It seemed as though I had lost all inspiration for self-expression. The work of others gave me no help, for there again it reflected only commercialism. And then one Sunday I saw your notice in the *Times* and decided to come and see an exhibition devoted entirely to non-objective painting. It was like a miracle to come here. It awakened every feeling which for so long had remained inactive, and it gave me new inspiration. Although I still do the same work for my living, I have begun to paint again for myself, and I find that I want to paint this way. Now I am beginning to free myself, to come alive again.

There isn't another museum that equals this one anywhere in New York – in fact, for me, there is not a greater museum anywhere. The first time I came here, several months ago, I could scarcely believe my eyes. I had never seen such beautiful paintings in such a lovely and inviting atmosphere. It had never occurred to me what a difference arrangement and lighting can make. I'm afraid I have become spoiled for any other type of exhibit. I think that Mr Guggenheim should have felt proud and happy that he was responsible for making such an outstanding museum possible, and accessible to everyone alike. To my mind, the Museum of Non-Objective Painting is a landmark in modern art, and it should serve as an example to all others who want to advance the culture of our time.

What an appealing little trio is the series of these three paintings by Nebel – *Compositions* 242, 243 and 246. The designs remind one of Chinese calligraphy. They have that same freedom and lack of mechanical imitation and repetition. Each of the paintings has rich colors and refinement. The mats and frames seem to be chosen with the same tasteful selection of the paintings. My, how I would love to own them.

This museum is a long-sought refuge. I dread to leave it. Here one feels serene and safe from the pressures of the world outside. I have never felt such a sense of peace in any place, other than my own home when I was a child. I wish I could take it with me always . . . this wonderful awareness of beauty and joy that I feel so strongly when I am in this museum.

I found myself carried away in space, and time was forgotten. It is unbelievable that such feelings can come to one through looking at a painting. I felt part of the great religion of all time; part of the creative force of the universe. These are not mere painted canvases, but part of cosmic truth, that is for all people to feel and find. We must not question loudly why or what, but shed all material intellectual opinions, and let the fluid warmth of beauty enter our being.

This is the loveliest museum I have ever seen in my life. The quiet informality, the music and flowers, the warmth of the atmosphere, and the unpretentiousness of the display are in perfect keeping with the idea of non-objective art. This art is so unfettered and direct. It opens up your heart to the purest instincts and needs. It presents itself modestly, yet with an inner strength which is stimulating.

This is a wonderful museum for the whole family. We have visited several times with our two youngsters, and it's amazing how well they behave here! I'm sure it's mainly because they genuinely love the paintings. They become filled with imagination and wonder. And the lovely atmosphere and quiet music gives this museum a less formal and cold air than the usual museum. Children sense these qualities immediately, and naturally warm up and respond to the pure beauty of this wonderful place.

Each visit here seems to add greatly to my aesthetic appreciation, not only of these paintings, but of other experiences in life. My responses have become sharpened; my inner consciousness awakened. These paintings have the power and magnetism to open one's soul like a flower.

APPENDIX IV
Questionnaire used in 1971 to obtain information about a number of museums in the German Federal Republic

This questionnaire, of which a translation is given below, was prepared and supervised by the Institute of Applied Consumer Research, Cologne, and the Institute for Comparative Social Research, Cologne. Replies were anonymous and the form had to be dealt with and handed in on the spot. Information was provided mainly by ringing the appropriate number in each section.

Members of the public were asked to co-operate 'in order to help to make museums even more attractive to visitors'. The helpfulness of some of the questions to museum administrators, curators and designers is not immediately apparent, but in Germany, as in the United States, surveys of this type are likely to be carried out with unrelenting thoroughness.

1   Name of museum

2   Place

3   Date

4   Period when the museum was visited:
    1 Morning
    2 Afternoon
    3 Evening

5   Approximate time visit began
    Approximate time visit ended

6   Sex
    1 Male
    2 Female

7   Age

8   Family status
    1   Single
    2   Married without children
    3   Married, with a child or children under 14
    4   Married, with a child or children over 14
    5   Widowed, formerly married
    5   Separated

9   What is your occupation? (Please state this precisely, especially in the case of clerical workers.)
Not employed
    1   Housewife. Please give your husband's occupation.
    2   Pensioner, private means. Please give your former occupation.
    3   Apprentice
    4   At school
    5   Student
    6   Soldier
Occupied as
    1   Manual worker
    2   Skilled worker
    3   Foreman, supervisor
    4   Clerical worker
    5   Higher clerical worker
    6   Clerical supervisor
    7   Civil servant, lower grade
    8   Civil servant, middle grade
    9   Civil servant, higher grade
   10   Professional, intellectual worker, e.g. doctor, lawyer
   11   Self-employed, lower and middle grade
   12   Self-employed, higher grade.

10   In which of the following fields do you (did you) or your husband work?
    1   Manufacturing industry
    2   Handicrafts
    3   Commerce
    4   Banking, credit
    5   Insurance

  6 Other service industry
  7 Entertainment, cultural pursuits
  8 Law, administration
  9 Health, medicine
10 Teaching
11 Agriculture
12 Other

11 What kind of educational establishment did you last attend?
  1 Primary school
  2 Middle school
  3 Secondary school, without leaving certificate (*Abitur*)
  4 Secondary school, with leaving certificate
  5 Technical school, without diploma
  6 Technical school, with diploma
  7 Technical college, university, without degree
  8 Technical college, university, with degree

12 Nationality
  1 German
  2 European (EEC)
  3 European (not EEC)
  4 Non-European

13 Where do you live?
  1 Here
  2 Within a radius of 60 km from here
  3 Further than 60 km from here

14 Do you work in this town or are you here for another reason?
  1 Work here
  2 A tourist, on holiday
  3 Visiting relatives
  4 Visiting friends, acquaintances
  5 For cultural reasons
  6 Other personal reasons

15 With whom did you come to the Museum?
  1 Alone
  2 With a member or members of my family

    3   With other relations
    4   With a friend or acquaintance
    5   With an organised group (e.g. school, association, works-party)
    6   With a tour

16   Why did you come to the Museum?
    1   A chance visit
    2   A general wish to see the Museum
    3   Because friends or acquaintances were coming
    4   On the recommendation of someone else
    5   To see a special exhibition
    6   I saw a poster, advertisement
    7   Report or notice in a newspaper or magazine
    8   I usually visit museums in new places
    9   To show my friends or relations the most interesting places in the city.
   10 Other reasons

17   Have you been to the Museum before, or is this your first visit?
    1   First visit
    2   Second visit
    3   Several times

18   Did you come to see particular exhibits or a special exhibition, or to look round the Museum as a whole?
    1   Particular exhibits
    2   Special exhibition
    3   Museum as a whole

19   If you have already ringed 18(1) or (2), did you see anything else in the Museum?
    1   Looked at other exhibits
    2   Looked at other exhibits in passing
    3   Looked at nothing else

20   Do you envisage visiting this Museum again in the near future?
    1   Yes
    2   No

21   How have you obtained information about the exhibits

which particularly interest you?
1 Before coming to the Museum
2 Through the exhibit-labels
3 Through a catalogue
4 Through other material provided by the museum (printed or recorded)
5 Through a book I brought with me
6 By going round with a guide or expert
7 No previous information

22 Thinking particularly about the information provided here in the Museum, would you say this was adequate, or would you have been grateful for more?
1 Adequate
2 Grateful for more

23 How did you find the display techniques?
1 Suitable, helpful
2 Unsuitable
3 Partly suitable, partly unsuitable

24 How frequently do you visit museums in general?
1 Whenever I have the opportunity
2 Frequently
3 Occasionally
4 Very seldom

25 What kind of museum do you particularly enjoy?
1 Art museums
2 Technical museums
3 Natural history museums
4 Local history museums
5 Museums of cultural history
6 Ethnographical museums
7 Other museums

26 How do you most like to visit a museum?
1 With an organised tour
2 With a knowledgeable friend or an expert
3 With someone with whom I can discuss what I see
4 Alone

NOTES

INTRODUCTION

[1] 'The Fault is in Ourselves', *Museums Journal*, vol. 64 no. 3 (Dec 1964) p. 227.
[2] Ibid., p. 229.
[3] Ibid., p. 228.
[4] In his introduction to Douglas Cooper's *Great Private Collections* (1963) p. 15.
[5] 'Le Rôle des Musées dans la Vie Moderne', *Revue des Deux Mondes*, 15 Oct 1937. See also Alma S. Wittlin, *The Museum: its history and its tasks in education* (1949) p. 133.
[6] 'Chronological Bibliography of Museum Visitor Surveys', *Museum News*, Feb 1964.
[7] G. T. Fechner, *Vorschule der Aesthetik*.

CHAPTER I

[1] *The Life of William Hutton, Stationer, of Birmingham, written by himself* (1841) p. 41. This is the second edition of a work first published in 1816. Conditions at the Museum improved between the first and second editions. Hutton's account of his visit, writes the 1841 edition, 'may make people the more sensible of the present facilities of access, and of the courtesy now shown to all classes by the officers and servants of that national establishment'.
[2] Ibid., p. 41. The German historian, Wendeborn, who managed to visit the British Museum in 1785, experienced even greater frustrations than those described by Hutton.
[3] The original constitution remained unchanged until 1963. The Chief Ministers of State were ex-officio Trustees, with the Lord Chancellor, the Archbishop of Canterbury and the Speaker of the House of Commons as Principal Trustees. The intention of these provisions was good, but in fact, both Ministers and Parliament soon ceased to take an informed interest in the Museum and effective control passed to the Civil Service, which saw to it that the Museum was always starved of funds.
[4] Originally published in his *Teutsche Academie der Edlen Bau-Bilde-und Mahlerei Kuenste* (1679). The English translation given here is from Mary F. S. Hervey's

Life, Correspondence and Collections of Thomas Howard, Earl of Arundel (1921).
5 Thomas Howard had inherited many fine portraits, including a number by Holbein, from his great-grandfather, Henry Fitzalan.
6 On this, see Hervey, op. cit., p. 140.
7 *The Voices of Silence* (1954) pp. 13–14.
8 Francis Haskell, *Patrons and Painters: a Study in the Relations between Italian Art and Society in the Age of the Baroque*, p. 9.
9 Quoted by Haskell, op. cit., p. 121.
10 Ibid., p. 129.
11 At another of the Society of Arts exhibitions, in 1761, eight constables were needed to control the crowd in a single room. Here, too, there was free admission.
12 Alma S. Wittlin, *Museums in Search of a Usable Future* (1970) p. 71.
13 Quoted by William T. Whitley, *Artists and their Friends in England, 1700–99* (1928) pp. 174–5.
14 i.e. Tahiti.
16 In *The Gentleman's Magazine*, vol. 18 (July 1748).
15 No. 34, Tuesday, 28 June 1709.
17 For the origins and development of the Society, see Lionel Cust, *History of the Society of Dilettanti* (1914).
18 More precisely, vol. 1 was published in that year.
19 Cust, op. cit., p. 81.
20 Especially those carried out by Sir William Hamilton, whose famous collection of Greek vases, terra-cottas, bronzes and gold ornaments was subsequently sold to the nation and formed the nucleus of the Department of Greek and Roman Antiquities in the British Museum.
21 Niels von Holst, *Creators, Collectors and Connoisseurs* (1967) p. 183.
22 Now in the Bibliothèque Nationale.
23 13 Sep 1773.
24 William T. Whitley, *Artists and their Friends in England, 1700–99*, Vol. 1 (1928) p. 28.
25 See John Steegman, *The Rule of Taste from George I to George IV* (1936) p. 107.
26 *The Rule of Taste*, p. 184.
27 *Works of Art and Artists in Britain*, trans. H. E. Lloyd, Vol. III (1838) pp. 3–4. Gustav Waagen was appointed Director of the newly established Royal Picture Gallery, Berlin in 1821, when he was twenty-five. During his 1835 tour of private and public art collections in Britain, he collected material for his list of 10,000 paintings. This was expanded during subsequent visits and was published in its final four-volume form in 1854, as *Treasures of Art in Great Britain*.
28 Ibid., pp. 90–1.

CHAPTER 2

1 Its history is outlined by Caroline M. Borowsky in *Museum News*, Feb 1963, pp. 11–21. See also Laura M. Bragg, 'The Birth of the Museum Idea in America', *Charleston Museum Quarterly*, 1 (1923) pp. 3–4.
2 June 1857.
3 See Richard P. Ellis, 'The Founding, History and Significance of Peale's Museum in Philadelphia, 1785–1841', in *Curator*, vol. 9 no. 3 (1966).

[4] Ellis, op. cit. The articles in *Curator* are not paginated.

[5] *Pennsylvania Packet*, 18 July 1786.

[6] Charles Willson Peale, *Letter-Book 2*, in the possession of the American Philosophical Society.

[7] *Dunlap's Daily American Advertiser*, 28 Aug 1792.

[8] For its origins and development, see Walter Muir Whitehill, *The East India Marine Society and the Peabody Museum of Salem: A Sesquicentennial History* (1949).

[9] Whitehill, op. cit., p. 45.

[10] Ibid., pp. 45–6.

[11] Gudrun Caloo, 'Museen und Sammler des 19 Jahrhunderts in Deutschland', *Museumskunde*, vol. 38 (1969) p. 59.

[12] *Dichtung und Wahrheit*, vol. 2 bk. 8.

[13] op. cit., pp. 80–1.

[14] op. cit., p. 185.

[15] 2 Aug 1850.

[16] 24 Mar 1851.

[17] 2 June 1851.

[18] The most important nineteenth-century exhibitions were London (1851, 1862, 1871), Paris (1867, 1878, 1889), Antwerp (1869), St Petersburg (1870), Moscow (1872), Vienna (1873), Philadelphia (1876) and Chicago (1893).

[19] *The Museum and Popular Culture* (1939) p. 10.

[20] 24 Jan 1851.

[21] 26 Aug 1851.

[22] *Journal of the Bath and West Society*, 1860. In the nineteenth century the great English houses were incomparably rich in works of art. The 1812 paintings shown at the Manchester Art Treasures exhibition, organised by G. F. Waagen in 1857 at the instigation of the Prince Consort, were drawn entirely from private sources. These loan collections were sent to the provinces in horse-drawn vans, by the Museum's Department of Circulation. The service is still very active today.

[23] Ibid., 1873, p. 44.

[24] Ibid., probably 1859, pp. 223–4.

[25] Ibid., 1870, p. 37. The aim of the Bath and West Society was, of course, based on those of the South Kensington Museum itself, which had to be envisaged in 1852 as an institution 'by which all classes might be induced to investigate those common principles of taste which may be traced in the works of excellence of all ages'.

[26] Ibid., p. 37.

[27] Ibid., pp. 37–8.

CHAPTER 3

[1] 'Design Standards in Museum Exhibits', *Curator*, no. 1 (1958), p. 29.

[2] For an account of its history and arrangement, see Arthur T. Bolton (ed.), *Description of the House and Museum on the North Side of Lincoln's Inn Fields, the Residence of Sir John Soane* (11th ed., 1930).

[3] *Popular Description of Sir John Soane's House, Museum and Library*.

[4] It is discussed by Niels von Holst, *Creators, Collectors and Connoisseurs* (1967) p. 229.

5 The practice had already been followed in the Musée Napoléon, in Paris.
6 Quoted in *National Museum of Ethnology, Leiden, 1837–1962*, published by the Museum in 1962, p. 4.
7 Ibid., p. 14. For a further discussion of the Museum's philosophy, see Peter H. Pott (Director of the Museum), 'The Role of Museums of History and Folklore in a Changing World', *Curator*, vol. 6 no. 2 (1963).
8 Harald von Petrikovits, Introduction to *150 Jahre Sammlungen des Rheinisches Landesmuseums Bonn* (1970).
9 *Essays on Museums*, p. 17.
10 Whitehill, Walter Muir, *The East India Marine Society and the Peabody Museum of Salem*, p. 126.
11 24 Nov 1869.
12 'Gustav Klemms Kulturhistorisches Museum', *Jahrbuch des Museums für Völkerkunde zu Leipzig*, Band XXVI (1964) p. 53.
13 Irmgard Woldering, 'Kestner Museum 1889–1964', *Hannoversche Geschichtsblätter*, new series, vol. 18 pt 2/4.
14 The Crown Princess, who was instrumental in getting the new museum established, was the daughter of Prince Albert.
15 'A National Art Museum for Germany', *The Times*, 22 Nov 1881.
16 'Designed for Use: the Cooper Union Museum', *Museum News*, Mar 1961.
17 *Museums and Art Galleries* (1888) pp. 319–20.
18 Ibid., p. 8. Greenwood was an outspoken opponent of the over-policing of museums. At the Natural History Museum in London he noted, p. 237, 'scores of young children apparently by themselves'; but that 'no one was needed to prevent injury to the cases or to keep them from touching the exhibits'.
19 Reported in *The Times*, 4 Aug 1880.
20 Greenwood, op. cit., pp. 173–4.
21 *Museums and Education*, 1968, v.
22 10 Sep.
23 Thomas Greenwood, *Museums and Art Galleries* (1888) p. 388.
24 *Museums: Their History and Use*, vol. I, (1904) p. 258.
25 On its history, see Wladislaw Rogala, 'The Contribution of the Polish Agricultural Museum to the Enhancement of Science and Agriculture in the Years 1875–1970', *Acta Muzeorum Agriculturae*, vol. 6 nos 1–2 (1971) pp. 85–93.
26 Rolf Kiau, 'Zur Entwicklung der Museen der DDR', *Neue Museumskunde*, Jahrgang 12, 4/1969, p. 429.
27 Kiau, op. cit., p. 456.
28 *The Museum: its history and its tasks in education*, pp. xiii–xiv.
29 *Changing Museums: Their Use and Misuse* (1967) p. ix.
30 'Museum History and Museum of History' (1904) p. 1.
31 *Changing Museums: Their Use and Misuse*, p. 27.
32 23 Nov 1874.
33 26 Nov 1874.
34 *The Times*, 2 Nov 1883.
35 *Museums and National Life* (Romanes Lecture, 1925) (1927) p. 20.
36 No. 5, 1901.

CHAPTER 4

[1] 'The Role of Museums of History and Folklore in a Changing World', *Curator*, vol. 6 no. 2 (1963).

[2] *Curator*, vol. 6 no. 1 (1963) p. 77.

[3] *Changing Museums: Their Use and Misuse*, p. 5.

[4] In a letter to *The Times*, 12 Mar 1974.

[5] *Le Musée de Dijon: sa Formation, son Développement*, p. 28.

[6] 'Museum and Art Gallery Buildings in England, 1845–1914', pt. II, *Museums Journal*, vol. 65 no. 4 (Mar 1966) p. 280.

[7] The experiment is described by R. van Luttervelt, *Dutch Museums* (1960) p. 62.

[8] December 23, 1852. Cleaning and restoration became steadily more necessary and urgent as industrialisation became more widespread. In Manchester, for example, the City Art Gallery found itself with an enormous conservation problem of weakened canvases and dirty frames as a result of the amount of carbon and sulphur in the dreadful atmosphere of the late nineteenth century.

[9] *The Times*, 2 Sep 1972.

[10] There are some interesting and surprisingly early thoughts about this in Laurence Vail Coleman, *The Museum in America*, vol. 1 (1939) p. 38.

[11] A. E. Parr, 'Problems of Museum Architecture', *Curator*, vol. 4 no. 4 (1961) p. 307.

[12] David B. Little, 'The Misguided Mission: a Disenchanted View of Art Museums Today', *Curator*, vol. 10 no. 3 (1967) pp. 221–2.

[13] Paul Marshall Rea, *The Museum and the Community* (1932) pp. 61–2.

[14] Ibid., p. 133.

[15] Dillon Ripley, *The Sacred Grove* (1969) pp. 107–8.

[16] 'Are Art Galleries Obsolete?' *Curator*, vol. 12 no. 1 (1969) p. 10.

[17] Ibid., p. 13.

[18] Charles J. Cornish, *Sir William Henry Flower: a Personal Memoir* (1904) p. 75.

[19] Published by the Museum in 1969.

[20] p. 21.

[21] p. 9.

[22] p. 2.

[23] p. 3.

[24] p. 4

[25] 'A great Museum Pioneer of the Nineteenth Century', *Curator*, vol. 7 no. 3 (1964) p. 333. The first open-air museum was, in fact, set up in the Netherlands, not in Sweden. It consisted of a number of houses from different parts of Indonesia, brought from the International Colonial Exhibition held in Amsterdam in 1883 and re-erected in 1885 on land belonging to the University. During the summer months these houses were furnished and peopled by plaster figures in native dress. To begin with it attracted a large public, but attendance soon fell off and by 1903 the site had been cleared. Skansen, which was opened in 1891, can therefore be considered the first permanent open-air museum.

[26] They have a manual of their own, Laurence Vail Coleman's *Historic House Museums*, published by the American Association of Museums in 1933.

[27] Niels von Holst, *Creators, Collectors and Connoisseurs* (1967) p. 294.

[28] *The Museum: q Manual of the Housing and Care of Art Collections* (1917) pp. 210–11.

[29] Ibid., p. 211.

[30] Quoted in his *Essays on Museums* (1898) p. 36.

[31] Ibid., p. 12.

CHAPTER 5

[1] 'Museum Audience Research', *Museum News*, Oct 1961, p. 34.

[2] This was before the collection was renamed in 1952.

[3] A more comprehensive selection of these comments is given below in Appendix III.

[4] 'Museum Audience Research', op. cit., p. 36.

[5] *The Museum in America*, vol. 2 (1939) p. 277.

[6] Ibid., p. 277.

[7] Her researches are described in *Behaviour of the Average Visitor in the Peabody Museum* (1938).

[8] 'Why Johnny Can't Read Labels', *Curator*, vol. 6 no. 2 (1963) p. 155.

[9] Ibid., p. 155.

[10] Described in Erwin V. Christensen, 'Labels for Masterpieces', *Museum News*, vol. 43 no. 9 (May 1965).

[11] Wallace N. MacBrian 'Testing Your Audience', *Museum News*, vol. 42 no. 8 (Apr 1964) p. 16.

[12] Ibid., pp. 16–17.

[13] Lee A. Parsons, 'Systematic Testing of Display Techniques for an Anthropoligical Exhibit', *Curator*, vol. 7 no. 2 (1965) p. 186.

[14] Ibid., p. 189.

[15] 'The Evaluation of Existing Criteria for Judging the Quality of Science Exhibits', *Curator*, vol. 11 no. 2 (1968).

[16] op. cit., p. 138.

[17] *The Sacred Grove* (1969) pp. 103–4.

[18] Vol. 68, nos. 1 and 2, June and Sep 1968.

[19] Doughty shows great sympathy with the views expressed by W. E. Washburn in 'The Museum's responsibility in Adult Education', *Curator*, vol. 7 no. 1 (1964).

[20] 'The Cult of the Known', *Museums Journal*, vol. 55 no. 6 (1955).

[21] 'Museum Function or Policy: a Comment on the Public of the Ulster Museum', *Museums Journal*, vol. 68 no. 4 (Mar 1969).

[22] His findings are outlined in 'The Belfast Public and the Ulster Museum', *Museums Journal*, vol. 70 no. 4 (Mar 1971).

[23] 'The Antiquities Gallery of Dundee Museum: a visitor survey', *Museums Journal*, vol. 70 no. 4 (Mar 1971).

[24] Published as *L'Amour de l'Art: les Musées et leur Public* (Paris, 1966).

[25] 7 Mar 1911.

[26] 7 Mar 1911.

[27] 3 June 1905.

[28] Aug 1905.

[29] Herbert Goldhammer, 'Über die systematische Entwicklung von differenzierten Formen und Methoden der Bildungs- und Erziehungsarbeit im Kunstmuseum', *Neue Museumskunde*, Jahren 14, 3/1971.

[30] For a more detailed analysis of this kind of museum and its problems, see Kenneth Hudson, 'How not to get information from a small museum', *ICOM News*, vol. 26 no. 2 (summer 1973).

[30] 'Reflections on MUSE', *Museum News* (May 1972) p. 12.

[31] Ibid., p. 13.

[32] Quoted in *National Museum of Ethnology, Leiden, 1837–1962*, published by the Museum in 1962, p. 4.

[33] Apr 1974, pp. 22–9.

BOOKS AND
ARTICLES CONSULTED

Abbey, D. S., and Cameron, Duncan F., 'The Museum Visitor: Survey Design' and 'The Museum Visitor: Survey Results', Royal Ontario Museum, 1960

Aellen, V., *159 Ans du Muséum d'Histoire Naturelle de Génève*, 1970

Barnaud, G., *Repertoire des Musées de France et de la Communauté*, 1959

Bayer, Herbert, 'Aspects of Design of Exhibitions and Museums', *Curator*, vol. 4 no. 3 (1961)

Bell, Whitfield J., et al., *A Cabinet of Curiosities: Five Episodes in the Evolution of American Museums* (intro. by W. M. Whitehill), 1967

Blair, James A. (ed.), *100 Years of Dundee Museums and Art Galleries, 1873–1973*, Dundee Museums and Art Galleries, 1973

von Bode, Wilhelm, *Mein Leben*, 2 vols, 1930

Bolton, Arthur T., *Description of the House and Museum on the North Side of Lincoln's Inn Fields, The Residence of Sir John Soane . . .* 11th ed., 1930

Borhegyi, Stephen F. de, 'Testing of Audience Reaction to Museum Exhibits', *Curator*, vol. 8 no. 1 (1965)

Borowsky, Caroline M., 'The Charleston Museum, 1773–1963', *Museum News*, Feb 1963

Bourdieu, Pierre, and Darbel, Alain, *L'Amour de l'Art: les Musées et leur Public*, Paris, 1966

Bragg, Laura M., 'The Birth of the Museum Idea in America', *Charleston Museum Quarterly*, 1 (1923)

100: The Buffalo Fine Arts Academy, 1862–1962, Albright-Knox Art Gallery, 1962

Burton, E. Milby, *South Carolina Silversmiths, 1690–1860* (Rut-land, Vermont: The Charles Tuttle Co., 1968)

Caloo, Gudrun, 'Museen und Sammler des 19 Jahrhunderts in Deutschland', *Museumskunde*, vol. 38 (1969)

Cameron, Duncan F., and Abbey, David S., 'Museum Audience Research: the Effect of an Admission Fee', *Museum News*, Nov 1963

Christensen, Erwin V., 'Labels for Masterpieces', *Museum News*, vol. 43 no. 9 (May 1965)

Coleman, Laurence Vail, *Historic House Museums*, 1933

Coleman, Laurence Vail, *The Museum in America*, vol. I, 1939

Cooper, Douglas (ed.), *Great Private Collections*, 1963

Cornish, Charles J., *Sir William Henry Flower: a Personal Memoir*, 1904

Coutts, Herbert, 'The Antiquities Gallery of Dundee Museum: a Visitor Survey', *Museums Journal*, vol. 70 no. 4 (Mar 1971)

Cox, Leonard, *The National Gallery of Victoria, 1861–1968: A Search for a Collection*, 1970

Crook, J. M., *The British Museum*, 1972

Cust, Lionel, *History of the Society of Dilettanti*, 1914

Dostal, Walter, 'Volksbildung und Völkerkundemuseum', *Neue Volksbildung*, Heft 10, 1957

Doughty, Philip S., 'The Public of the Ulster Museum: a Statistical Survey', *Museums Journal*, vol. 68 no. 2 (Sep 1968)

Eckhardt, Wolfgang, 'Das Museum für Kunst und Gewerbe Hamburg', *Weltkunst*, XLI, Jahrgang no. 13 (July 1971)

Egg, E., '150 Jahre Tiroler Landesmuseum Ferdinandeum', *Veröffertlichungen des Tiroler Landesmuseum Ferdinandeum*, Band 53, Jahrgang 1973

Ellis, Richard P., 'The Founding, History and Significance of Peale's Museum in Philadelphia, 1785–1841', *Curator*, vol. 9 no. 3 (1966)

Erwin, David G., 'The Belfast Public and the Ulster Museum: a Statistical Survey', *Museums Journal*, vol. 70 no. 4 (Mar 1971)

Fechner, G. T., *Vorschule der Aesthetik*, 1897

Fellenberg, Edward von, *Ein Gang durch das städtliche Antiquarium in Bern*, 1876

Feuchtmüller, Mrazek, *Kunst in Österreich, 1860–1918*, 1964

Finlay, Ian, 'What Image? What Public?', *Museums Journal*, vol. 64 no. 3 (Dec 1964)

Finnberg, J., *Turun kaupungen historiallinen museo, 1881–1931*, 1932

The First Hundred Years of the Museum, South Australian Museum (undated)

Fitzinger, Leopold Josef, *Geschichte des Kais. Kon. Hof-Naturalien Cabinets zu Wien*, 1856

Flower, Sir William Henry, *Essays on Museums*, 1898

Fraser, Ross, 'The Gallery's First Eighty Years', *Quarterly* of the Auckland City Art Gallery, no. 49 (Mar 1971)

Geschichte der Kunstgesellschaft Luzern, 1920

Gibbs-Smith, Charles H., 'The Fault . . . is . . . in Ourselves', *Museums Journal*, vol. 64 no. 3 (Dec 1964)

Gibbs-Smith, Charles H., and Dougharty, K., *History of the Victoria and Albert Museum*, 1952

Goldhammer, Herbert, 'Über die systematische Entwicklung von differenzierten Formen und Methoden der Bildungs- und Erziehungsarbeit in Kunstmuseum', *Neue Museumskunde*, Jahrgang 14, 3/1971

Gould, Cecil, 'Some Thoughts on the Design of Picture Galleries and the Hanging of Pictures', *Museums Journal*, vol. 68 no. 1 (1968)

Greenaway, F., *Short History of the Science Museum*, 1953

Greenwood, Thomas, *Museums and Art Galleries*, 1888

'Gustav Klemms Kulturhistorisches Museum', *Jahrbuch des Museums für Völkerkunde zu Leipzig*, Band XXVI, 1964

Harden, D. B., 'The Cult of the Known', *Museums Journal*, vol. 55 no. 6, 1955

Harrison, Molly, *Changing Museums: Their Use and Misuse*, 1967

Harvey, E. D., and Friedberg, Bernard L. (eds), *A Museum for the People*, 1971

Haskell, Francis, *Patrons and Painters: a Study in the Relations between Italian Art and Society in the Age of the Baroque*, 1963

Hathaway, Calvin S., 'Designed for Use: the Cooper Union Museum', *Museum News*, Mar 1961

Heim, Roger, and Laissus, Yves, 'Le Muséum National d'Histoire Naturelle', *Revue de l'Enseignements Supérieur*, no. 2, 1962

Hervey, Mary F. S., *The Life, Correspondence and Collections of Thomas Howard, Earl of Arundel, 'Father of Vertu in England'*, 1921

Hezekiah, Lloyd, 'Reflections on MUSE', *Museum News*, May 1972

Hightower, John B., 'Are Art Galleries Obsolete?' *Curator*, vol. 12 no. 1 (1969)

'History of Museums in the United States: report of a session of the American Historical Association', *Curator*, vol. 8 no. 1 (1965)

Hjelte, R., 'Vilka går på museum? En ondersökning av Nordiska museets publik', *Svenska Museer*, 1954, 3–4, 1955, 1.

von Holst, Niels, *Creators, Collectors and Connoisseurs*, 1967

Hudson, Kenneth, 'How not to get information from a small museum', *ICOM News*, vol. 26 no. 2 (summer 1973)

Hutton, William, *The Life of William Hutton, Stationer, of Birmingham*, 2nd ed., 1841

Huyge, René, 'Le Rôle des Musées dans la Vie Moderne', *Revue des Deux Mondes*, 15 Oct 1937

Jackson, Margaret Talbot, *The Museum: a Manual of the Housing and Care of Art Collections*, 1917

Jones, Joyce, 'Museum and Art Gallery Buildings in England, 1845–1914', *Museums Journal*, vol. 65 no. 4 (Mar 1966)

Karlin, Georg J:son, *Kulturhistorisk Förening och Museum i Lund*, 1932

Key, Archie F., 'Canada's Museum Explosion: The First One Hundred Years', *Museums Journal*, vol. 67 no. 1 (June 1967)

Kiau, Rolf, 'Zur Entwicklung der Museen der DDR', *Neue Museumskunde*, 4/1969

Klein, Rudolf, 'Who goes to museums?', *Illustrated London News*, Apr 1974

Kogan, Herman, *A Continuing Marvel: history of the Museum of Science and Industry, Chicago*, 1973

Lagercrantz, Bo, 'A Great Museum Pioneer of the Nineteenth Century', *Curator*, vol. 7 no. 3 (1964)

Larrabee, Eric (ed.), *Museums and Education*, 1968

Lerman, Leo, *The Museum: One Hundred Years of the Metropolitan Museum of Art*, 1969

Lhotsky, A., *Festschrift des Kunsthistorischen Museums*, 2 Teil: Die Geschichte der Sammlungen Wien, 1941–5

Little, David B., 'The Misguided Mission: a Disenchanted View of Art Museums Today', *Curator*, vol. 10 no. 3 (1967)

van Luttervelt, R., *Dutch Museums*, 1960

MacBrian, Wallace N., 'Testing Your Audience', *Museum News*, vol. 42 no. 8 (Apr 1964)

Malkowsky, Georg, *Die Kunst im Dienste der Staatsidee* (Grosser Kurfürst bis Wilhelm II), 1912

Malraux, André, *The Voices of Silence*, 1954

The Mariners Museum, 1930–50: a history and guide, The Mariners Museum, Newport News, Virginia, 1950

McLuhan, Marshall, *et al.*, *Exploration of the Ways, Means, and Values of Museum Communication with the Viewing Public*, Seminar (1967) at the Museum of the City of New York, 1969

Mihalache, C., *Muzeele dm Bucurest*, 1960

Millar, Oliver, *Zoffany and his Tribuna*, 1967

Miller, Edward, *That Noble Cabinet* [i.e. the British Museum], 1974

Morrison, F. R., 'The Museum of Applied Arts and Sciences, Sydney', *Australian Journal of Science*, vol. 24 no. 12 (June 1962)

Murray, David, *Museums: their History and Use*, vol. 1, 1904

'Museums and the Eighteenth Century: a symposium held by the South Midlands Federation, 25th October 1958', *Museums Journal*, vol. 59 (Apr 1959–Mar 1960)

National Museum of Ethnology, Leiden, 1837 1962, 1962

Neal, Arminta, 'Gallery and Case Exhibit Design', *Curator*, vol. 6 no. 1 (1963)

Das Österreichische Museum für Völkskunde. Werden und Wesen eines Wiener Museums 1960

Pallat, Ludwig, *Richard Schöne, Generaldirektor der Kgl. Museen zu Berlin* (Kunstverwallung 1872–1905), 1959

Palomar, Francisco A., *Primeros Salones de Arte en Buenos Aires*, 2nd ed., 1972

Parker, Harley W., 'The Museum as a Communication System', *Curator*, vol. 6 no. 4 (1963)

Parr, A. E., 'Patterns of Progress in Exhibition', *Curator*, vol. 5 no. 4 (1962)

Parr, A. E., 'Problems of Museum Architecture', *Curator*, vol. 4 no. 4 (1961)

Parsons, Lee A., 'Systematic Testing of Display Techniques for an Anthropological Exhibit', *Curator*, vol. 8 no. 2 (1965)

Pickman, David, 'The Museum of Fine Arts, Boston: The First One Hundred Years', *Curator*, vol. 12 no. 4 (1969)

Plagemann, Volker, 'Die Anfänge der Hamburger Kunstsammlungen und die Erste Kunsthalle', *Jahrbuch der Hamburger Kunstsammlungen*, Band II, 1966

Plagemann, Volker, *Das deutsche Kunstmuseum, 1790–1870*, 1967

Poch-Kalous, M., *Die Gemäldegalerie der Akademie der Bildenden Künste in Wien*, 1968

Pope, Alexander, *Moral Essays*, Ep. IV

Porter, Mildred C. B., *Behavior of the Average Visitor in the Peabody Museum*, 1938

Pott, Peter H. 'The Roles of History and Folklore in a Changing World', *Curator*, vol. 6 no. 2 (1963)

Pycraft, W. P., *The British Museum of Natural History (South Kensington)*, 1910

Quarré, Pierre, *Le Musée de Dijon: Sa Formation, Son Développement*, 1950

Ramsey, Grace Fisher, *Educational Work in Museums in the United States*, 1938

Rea, Paul Marshall, *The Museum and the Community*, 1932

Das Rheinische Landesmuseum Bonn, 3–6/1970

's Rijks Museum van Natuurlijke Historie, Leiden 1918

Ripley, Dillon, *The Sacred Grove*, 1969

Rogala, Wladyslaw, 'The Contribution of the Polish Agricultural Museum to the Enhancement of Science and Agriculture in the Years 1875–1970', *Acta Muzeorum Agriculturae*, vol. 6 nos 1–2 (1971)

Sayles, Adelaide B., *The Story of the Children's Museum of Boston*, 1937

Scholler, Hubert, *Naturhistorisches Museum in Wien. Die Geschriebe der Wiener Naturhistorischen Sammlungen*, 1958

Schöndube, Wilhelm, and Steinbacher, Joachim, 'Aus der 150 jährigen Geschichte der Senckenbergischen Naturforschender Gesellschaft zu Frankfurt am Main', *Natur und Museum*, Band 97, Heft 11 (Nov 1967)

The Science Museum: The First Hundred Years, 1957

Shetelig, Haakon, *Norske Museens Historie*, 1944

Shettel, Harris H., 'An Evaluation of Existing Criteria for Judging the Quality of Science Exhibits', *Curator*, vol. 11 no. 2 (1968)

Sizer, C. A., 'Museum Function or Policy: a Comment on the Public at the Ulster Museum', *Museums Journal*, vol. 68 no. 4 (Mar 1969)

Steegman, John, *The Rule of Taste from George I to George IV*, 1936

Strahm, H., *Die Anfänge der naturhistorischen sammlungen in der alten*

Berner Stadt-bibliotek, Berner Zeitschrift für Geschichte und Heimatkunde, 1945

Taylor, Francis Henry, *The Taste of Angels: a History of Art Collecting from Rameses to Napoleon*, 1948

Tompkins, Calvin, *Merchants and Masterpieces: the Story of the Metropolitan Museum of Art*, 1970

Veikko, Anttila, *Suomen kotiseuduntutkimus 1894–1920 ja kansanperinteen joukkokeruun alkuhistoria*, 1964

Waagen, G. F., *Works of Art and Artists in England*, trans. H. E. Lloyd, 1838

Wactzoldt, W., 'Preussische Kunstpolitik und Kunstverwaltung, 1817–1932', *Reichsverwaltungsblatt*, Band 54, no. 5 (1933)

Wagner, Walter, 'Zur Entstehung der Landesmuseen in Österreich: ein Provinzialmuseum als Preisaufgabe an der Wiener Akademie der Bildenden Künste im Jahre 1824', *Museums Kunde*, 1/1968

Washburn, W. E., 'The Museum's Responsibility in Adult Education', *Curator*, vol. 8 no. 1 (1964)

Wegeli, R., '50 Jahre Bernisches Historisches Museum', *Jahrbuch des Bernischen Historischen Museums*, 1943

Weiner, George, 'Why Johnny Can't Read Labels', *Curator*, vol. 6 no. 2 (1963)

Whitehill, Walter Muir, *The East India Marine Society and the Peabody Museum of Salem: a Sesquicentennial History*, 1949

Whitehill, Walter Muir, *Museum of Fine Arts, Boston: a Centennial History*, 1970

Whitley, William T., *Artists and their Friends in England, 1700–99* vol. I, 1928

Willoch, S., *Nasjonalgalleriet gjennem hundre år*, 1937

Witteborg, Lothar P., 'Design Standards in Museum Exhibits', *Curator* (1958)

Wittke, Carl, *The First Fifty Years: The Cleveland Museum of Art, 1916–1966*, 1968

Wittlin, Alma S., *The Museum: its History and its Tasks in Education*, 1949

Wittlin, Alma S., *Museums in Search of a Usable Future*, 1970

Woldering, Irmgard, 'Kestner Museum, 1889–1964', *Hannoversche Geschichtsblätter*, Band 18, Heft 2/4, 1965

Woodward, Bernard H., 'The Western Australian Museum and Art Gallery, Perth', *Museums Journal* (Dec 1903)

Wüthricht, .L., *Schweizerisches Landesmuseum gestern-heute:* 75 *Jahre im Dienst der Öffentlichkeit*, Zurich, 1973

'Zum hundertjährigen Bestehen 1869–1969', *Jahrbuch des Museums für Völkerkunde zu Leipzig*, Band XXVI, 1969

Zygulski, Kazimierz, *Reception of Painting in Polish Museums (A qualitative analysis)*, Polish National Committee of ICOM, Poznan-Warszawa, 1974

INDEX